A gift for

from

ON
THIS
DAY
IN
HISTORY

ON THIS DAY IN HISTORY

GRAEME DONALD

Michael O'Mara Books Limited

First published in Great Britain in 2014 by
Michael O'Mara Books Limited
9 Lion Yard
Tremadoc Road
London SW4 7NQ

A CIP catalogue record for this book is available from the British Library.

Papers used by Michael O'Mara Books Limited are natural, recyclable products made from wood grown in sustainable forests. The manufacturing processes conform to the environmental regulations of the country of origin.

ISBN: 978-1-78243-216-6 in hardback print format
ISBN: 978-1-78243-270-8 in e-book format

2 3 4 5 6 7 8 9 10

www.mombooks.com

Designed and typeset by Billy Waqar

Printed and bound by CPI Group (UK) Ltd, Croydon, CR0 4YY

For Rhona – the best date I ever made!

FOREWORD

For a book of such self-explanatory structure a foreword might seem a trifle superfluous but it should be said that deciding what not to include presented the most difficult choices.

For example, history is peppered with natural disasters, so their mention was restricted to only those of global import to prevent the book becoming a catalogue of such events. Much the same censorship was imposed on the two World Wars and other major conflicts. Some of the characters mentioned in the following pages will be familiar to many readers, so only their lesser-known activities and proclivities are included. And some persons and events may surprise.

Perhaps inevitably, many of the dates themselves presented a quandary; for example, events in space that took place early on the morning of, say, 5 June on GMT, could be presented as late on 4 June at the American launch-site; which to choose? GMT was eventually taken as the benchmark.

At the end of the day, the book was constructed to afford the reader an interesting and informative day-by-day trawl through the centuries; all involved in the book's production hope you will find it so.

GRAEME DONALD

1

404

The last gladiatorial games are staged in Rome. The Games evolved from the funeral of Brutus in 264BC when men fought to the death to provide him with an escort in the afterlife.

1660

English naval administrator Samuel Pepys begins his famous diary with 'Blessed be God'.

1772

With the rich indulging in their Grand Tours of Europe, the London Credit Exchange issues the first traveller's cheques.

1892

Fifteen-year-old Annie Moore from Ireland becomes the first immigrant to be processed by the facilities on America's Ellis Island.

1934

Alcatraz ceases to be a military prison when it is formally signed over to the civil prison authorities. Although notorious for its tough conditions, the 600-cell complex never holds more than 300 prisoners and by the time it closes in 1963 is considered a luxury stay by some inmates.

1959

After six years of strife, President Batista flees Cuba, which now falls to the forces of Fidel Castro and Ernie Guevara Lynch, better known today as Che Guevara.

1492

Arab control of Spain ends with the fall of Granada, the Moors' last stronghold. 'Blue-blooded' was coined by the Spanish nobility during the occupation to distinguish themselves from the invaders, whose dark skin prevented their veins from showing blue at the wrist.

1757

Robert Clive recaptures the British fort at Calcutta, India, from the Nawab of Bengal and learns the fate of British captured by the Nawab's troops: allegedly, of 146 British men and women imprisoned overnight in a tiny cell, 123 had died by morning in the stifling heat.

1833

Britain asserts sovereignty over the Falkland Islands.

1955

José Remón Cantera, President of Panama, is assassinated.

1959

Soviets launch Luna 1, the first craft to get to the Moon, where it establishes the absence of any magnetic field.

1979

New York trial of Sex Pistols' singer, Sid Vicious, for the murder of his girlfriend, Nancy Spungen, in Greenwich Village. While on bail, he takes a fatal overdose.

3
JANUARY

1868

Japan brings down the curtain on centuries of military rule as the Shogunate is replaced by the sixteen-year-old Emperor, Meiji.

1917

British physicist Sir Ernest Rutherford announces that he has split the atom.

1922

Howard Carter enters the burial chamber of Egyptian pharaoh Tutankhamun. Following several 'mysterious' deaths, the media reports a curse on anyone who disturbs the tomb, which is enough to frighten off the locals and would-be grave-robbers. No such inscription existed, either on the walls or on any artefact.

1925

Mussolini announces he is assuming the Dictatorship of Italy.

1967

Having killed Lee Harvey Oswald (the sniper who assassinated President John F. Kennedy), Jack Ruby himself dies in a Dallas hospital of natural causes.

1980

Conservationist Friederike Victoria Gessner, aka Joy Adamson, author of *Born Free*, is found murdered near her Kenyan home.

4
JANUARY

1809/13

The respective birthdays of two famous 'code' writers – Louis Braille and Isaac Pitman. Braille based his system for the visually impaired on an invention of Charles Barbier, a French Army officer, who had devised night writing for the distribution of orders among soldiers without having to use lanterns.

1847

The Texas Rangers give Samuel Colt his first order when they commission 1,000 of his new revolvers, soon to be advertised as The Equalizer.

1958

After circling the earth for about three months, the first artificial earth satellite Sputnik 1 succumbs to orbit-decay and crashes back to earth.

1960

Donald Campbell dies trying to break the water-speed record on Coniston Water in northern England. His body is not found until 2001.

2010

Dubai's towering Burj Khalifa opens its doors as the world's tallest building.

5

1781

In the American War of Independence, Richmond, Virginia, is put to the torch by a British force led by the American traitor, Benedict Arnold.

1896

Wilhelm Röntgen makes public his discovery of X-rays.

1919

Munich sees the registering of a new political faction, The National Socialist German Workers' Party, led by an unemployed plumber called Anton Drexler; member 55 will be Adolf Hitler, who will later take over.

1925

Mrs Nellie Tayloe Ross of Wyoming becomes America's first female State Governor.

1930

Stalin institutes his disastrous Collectivization of Farms across the Soviet Union.

1941

British aviator Amy Johnson crashes and dies in the Thames Estuary.

1975

The Khmer Rouge mounts an all-out and successful offensive on Phnom Penh and rebrands Cambodia as Democratic Kampuchea.

6
JANUARY

1066
Harold accepts the English crown, breaking his deal with William of Normandy and opening the door to the most complete Viking invasion of England, as William and his Norsemen (Normans) defeat Harold, not at Hastings, but at Senlac Hill, about six miles away.

1540
Henry VIII takes Anne of Cleves as his fourth wife. Branding her 'The Flanders Mare', Henry soon casts her aside but she will outlive him.

1907
The first woman to graduate from an Italian Medical College, Maria Montessori, employs revolutionary teaching methods in her first school that opens today in Rome.

1929
The Albanian Agnes Bojaxhiu arrives in Calcutta to begin work as Mother Teresa.

1994
On the eve of the US Figure Skating Championships, Nancy Kerrigan is clubbed across the knees in Detroit's Cobo Arena by Shane Stant. Stant was working in collusion with Jeff Gillooly, the ex-husband of Kerrigan's main skating rival, Tonya Harding.

7

JANUARY

1558

The French drive the English out of Calais and reclaim the region.

1598

Boris Godunov seizes the Russian throne.

1610

Galileo discovers the moons of Jupiter but mistakes them for stars. The four moons are later named, Io, Europa, Callisto and Ganymede.

1789

The voting opens for the first presidential election of the newly independent United States of America – George Washington beats John Adams by sixty-nine votes to thirty-four.

1904

The Marconi Company announce CQD as a distress signal to be used worldwide. Like its replacement, SOS, it did not actually stand for anything. CQD was last transmitted by RMS *Titanic*.

1989

Having been forced publicly to renounce his divine status as a God-Ruler at the close of the Second World War, Japanese Emperor Hirohito dies today to be replaced by his son, Akihito.

1877
Chief 'His Horse is Crazy' (popularly known as 'Crazy Horse') and his warriors line up for their last battle against the United States Cavalry at Wolf Mountain in Montana.

1889
Herman Hollerith patents his first punch-card data gathering machine and forms the company that will evolve into IBM.

1904
Pope Pius X bans the wearing of low-cut dresses in the presence of clergy.

1912
The African National Congress is formed in South Africa.

1926
The Kingdom of the Hejaz invites Ibn Saud to assume complete power, which he does, renaming his new domain Saudi Arabia.

2011
Obsessed with Arizona Congresswoman Gabrielle Giffords, Jared Lee Loughner stalks her to the Safeway supermarket in Casas Adobes outside Tucson where he shoots her in the head before turning his gun on the crowd, killing six and injuring fourteen before being wrestled to the ground.

9

1799
Promised as a temporary measure to fund the Napoleonic Wars, British PM William Pitt the Younger introduces income tax.

1861
The first shots of the American Civil War are fired on the Northern ship, *Star of the West*, as it tries to land supplies for Fort Sumter, itself soon to be attacked.

1876
Henry Morton Stanley today colludes with King Leopold of Belgium to mount a land-grab of the Congo under the guise of a philanthropic mission, led by Stanley.

1909
Ernest Shackleton's South Pole venture stalls when he is forced to turn back after getting within 100 miles (160 km) of his goal.

1920
The Bolsheviks defeat the last vestige of White Russian opposition.

1923
Piloted by Alejandro Spencer, the world's first autogyro flies at Cuatro Vientos Airfield, Madrid.

1929
Alexander Fleming uses penicillin for the first time to treat an infection in his assistant, Stuart Craddock.

10
JANUARY

1806
Having defeated the Dutch at the Battle of Blaauwberg, the British take control of South Africa's Cape Colony.

1863
The Paddington Line, the first service on the London Underground, is opened by Prime Minister Gladstone.

1917
Self-made legend Buffalo Bill Cody dies peacefully in bed, surrounded by friends and family.

1918
The American House of Representatives allows votes for women – but only those who are over thirty and married.

1920
The League of Nations is formed and sits in council for the first time six days later in Paris as the terms of the Treaty of Versailles are put into effect to officially end the First World War.

1984
General Zia of Pakistan authorizes the release from prison of Benazir Bhutto, daughter of Prime Minister Zulfikar Ali Bhutto whom Zia had executed in 1979. Within four years she will be running the country but was herself assassinated in 2007.

11
JANUARY

1693
Mount Etna erupts as a powerful earthquake destroys large parts of Sicily and Malta.

1787
William Herschel is the first to observe Uranus and name its two newly discovered moons, Titania and Oberon.

1867
The left-wing revolutionary, Benito Juárez, after whom Benito Mussolini was named, returns in triumph to Mexico City as the ousted Emperor Maximilian faces a firing squad.

1879
The Anglo-Zulu War begins.

1922
At the Toronto General Hospital, fourteen-year-old Leonard Thompson becomes the first diabetic to be successfully treated with insulin by Dr Frederick Banting.

1974
The first sextuplets to all survive are born to Susan and Colin Rosenkowitz in Cape Town, South Africa.

1990
China finally lifts the martial law restriction put in place in the wake of the Tiananmen Square protests.

12

JANUARY

1904

Henry Ford establishes a new land-speed record of 91.37 mph (147.04 kph) in his car, 999, on Detroit's frozen Lake St Clair.

1908

The first long-range radio messages are sent from the top of the Eiffel Tower, Paris.

1964

Zanzibar ousts the draconian Sultan and re-brands itself a republic called Tanzania.

1971

Anti-war activists, the so-called Harrisburg Seven, go on trial for their alleged plan to kidnap US Security Advisor Henry Kissinger and blow up several Federal buildings. They are acquitted, but the trial is famous for its being the first to permit jury selection through the use of demographics and pre-trial questioning.

1977

Abu Daoud, the man who planned the Munich Olympics Massacre, flies into Paris from Beirut using a false passport.

2010

The Haitian capital, Port-au-Prince, is razed by a 7-magnitude earthquake which kills around 230,000 and leaves another 1.3 million homeless.

13
JANUARY

1898

Émile Zola publishes *J'Accuse*, his damning indictment of the anti-Semitic conspiracy that framed the Jewish Captain Alfred Dreyfus for treason.

1953

The newly constituted State of Yugoslavia chooses Marshal Tito as its first president.

1957

Inspired by a swathe of UFO 'sightings' and the well-known habit of Yale students to use the packaging plates of the Frisbee Pie Company as a projectile in campus games, the Wham-O Company markets the first purpose-made frisbees.

1969

Cannon and other items from Captain Cook's *Endeavour* are salvaged from the waters off Australia's Cooktown.

1978

For the first time in its history, NASA advertises for women to join up as mission specialists.

1992

Japan issues a long-overdue apology to the thousands of so-called Comfort Women of China, Korea and the Philippines who were forced to work in brothels set up specifically for Imperial troops during the Second World War.

14
JANUARY

1742

Sir Edmond Halley dies today. He is not the first to note the comet bearing his name – this has been recorded since 240BC – but he is the first to recognize its appearance as periodic and fix its earthly orbit at approximately 75 years.

1814

London hosts its last Frost Fair on the frozen River Thames; the general rise in temperatures is already making such frolics a thing of the past.

1878

The telephone is demonstrated to Queen Victoria at Osborne House and she immediately commissions installations throughout the British royal residences.

1907

Kingston in Jamaica is hit by a 6.5-magnitude earthquake. Between the quake and the resultant tsunamis, about 1,000 are killed and 10,000 are left homeless.

1963

French President Charles de Gaulle stands up at the Paris Conference and utters his famously monosyllabic 'Non!' to the suggestion that Britain be admitted to the European Economic Community.

15
JANUARY

1790

John Hetherington is arrested in London for wearing 'a tall structure on his head, calculated to frighten persons of a timid disposition'. The debut of the top hat.

1790

Fletcher Christian and his fellow mutineers from the *Bounty* arrive at Pitcairn Island in the Pacific Ocean.

1889

The Pemberton Medicine Company starts trading in Atlanta, Georgia, where its main product, Pemberton's Brain Tonic, will soon be re-branded as Coca-Cola.

1919

The Great Boston Molasses Flood. The first injuries are caused by people being 'shot' by the rivets being fired out of the rupturing tanks holding millions of gallons of molasses.

1973

President Nixon calls a halt to American offensive action in North Vietnam.

2009

Shortly after take-off at La Guardia, US Airways Flight 1549 hits a flock of birds and, with both engines seriously impaired, ditches in New York's Hudson River; all aboard survive.

16
JANUARY

27BC
Octavian accepts the title of Augustus to become the First Roman Emperor, a title never held by Julius Caesar.

1547
Ivan the Terrible is crowned First Tsar of All the Russians. His epithet was actually Ivan Grozny, which translates as Ivan the Awful, as in worthy of awe.

1581
Catholicism is declared illegal in England, so starting the fashion for priest holes in some of the larger houses to hide the celebrants of Mass in case of a raid.

1707
Scotland ratifies the Act of Union, which removes the last obstacle to the creation of Great Britain.

1793
The first free settlers arrive in Australia aboard the *Bellona*, five years after the first convicts were landed.

1967
The first all-black Government of The Bahamas is sworn in today.

2005
Romanian novelist, Adriana Iliescu, gives birth at the age of sixty-six, so becoming the world's oldest authenticated mother.

17
JANUARY

1377

The Papal Throne is moved back to Rome from Avignon.

1893

The Last Queen of Hawaii is deposed by a consortium of American and European businessmen prior to annexation with the United States.

1912

British explorer Captain Scott reaches the South Pole, only to realize that a Norwegian expedition has beaten him to it.

1920

Prohibition is instituted in the US today. Altar wine being exempt, priests suddenly find a need for an extra 800,000 gallons in the first two years of Prohibition.

1950

The Great Brinks Robbery; eleven men steal over $2.7 million from that company's Boston depository.

1966

A B-52 bomber with a full nuclear load collides with its re-fuelling plane in Spanish airspace. Both planes crash, with three of the four nuclear bombs landing around the tourist resort of Palomares. The fourth is lost at sea and not recovered for months.

18

1485

The Tudor Houses of York and Lancaster unite through the marriage of Henry VII of England to Elizabeth, daughter of Edward IV. Their recent conflict becomes known as The War of the Roses after the white and red rose emblems of the two Houses.

1778

Captain Cook discovers an island group and calls them the Sandwich Islands in honour of his main sponsor, John Montagu the 4th Earl of Sandwich, also the man who gave his name to the snack.

1871

At Versailles, Wilhelm of Prussia is proclaimed the First German Emperor; in less than fifty years the Germans will be back at Versailles to sign the treaty that officially ends the First World War.

1911

The first successful landing of a plane on a moving ship – piloting a Curtiss biplane, Eugene Ely lands on the converted cruiser, the USS *Pennsylvania*, as it traverses San Francisco Bay.

1967

Albert DeSalvo, aka The Boston Strangler, is convicted of thirteen murders and sent to prison for life, only to escape a few weeks later. He surrendered to his lawyer and was later stabbed to death in his cell.

19
JANUARY

1870

Feminist Victoria Woodhull opens the first all-female stock-brokerage on Wall Street, New York City, and, in 1872, becomes the first woman to run for president.

1903

With France still divided by the Dreyfus Affair, the anti-Semitic rag *L'Auto* announces its sponsorship of a new race – the Tour de France – so the pro-Dreyfus paper, *Le Vélo*, sets up a counter team. The newspapers were printed on yellow and green paper respectively, hence the colour of the jerseys worn by the stage and overall winners.

1915

Britain is bombed for the first time by Zeppelins over Great Yarmouth and King's Lynn.

1920

The US Senate votes against joining the League of Nations.

1949

Cuba votes to be one of the first to recognize the new State of Israel.

1966

Indira Gandhi becomes the first female prime minister of India.

1977

For the first time in recorded history, snow falls on Miami, Florida.

20
JANUARY

1265

The first sitting of the English Parliament in Westminster Hall, London. The adversarial seating arrangements are inspired by the fact that the first unofficial meetings took place in the choir-stalls of St Stephen's Chapel. The front benches are two-and-a-half sword-lengths apart to prevent heated debate getting bloody.

1841

Hong Kong cedes to the British during the First Opium War, a conflict arising when China tries to block the massive imports of opium from British colonies.

1878

An ancient Egyptian obelisk is erected on the Embankment of the River Thames, London. It comes to be known as Cleopatra's Needle, despite it pre-dating the lady by some 1,400 years. The name is shared by two other Egyptian obelisks erected in the nineteenth century, one in New York and one in Paris.

1942

In a quiet suburb of Berlin called Wannsee, Nazi SS officer Reinhard Heydrich hosts a conference to agree the structure of the Final Solution to the so-called Jewish Problem.

1981

After 444 days held captive, the fifty-two American hostages held after the attack on the US Embassy in Tehran in November 1979 are released by Iran.

21
JANUARY

1189
King Richard I of England (the Lionheart) initiates the Third Crusade to reconquer the Holy Land from Saladin.

1793
In France, Louis XVI is guillotined before a baying mob.

1799
A smallpox vaccine developed by English physician and scientist Edward Jenner is released for use. Jenner was not the first to make the connection between cowpox and smallpox. Country folk have known for centuries that anyone catching the former, known as Milkmaids' Grace, is immune to the latter.

1908
The City of New York makes it illegal for women to smoke in public.

1950
Author George Orwell dies today. He never knew of the Central Intelligence Agency's involvement in his work. The famous animated adaptation of his *Animal Farm*, made in black-and-white in 1954, was partly funded by the CIA in order to ridicule the Communists during the Cold War.

1977
President Carter proclaims amnesty for all those who fled the United States or hid out to evade the draft for the war in Vietnam.

22
JANUARY

1666
Mogul Emperor of India Shah Jahan, the man who built the Taj Mahal, dies under house arrest in Agra Fort, locked away by his own son.

1788
'Mad, bad and dangerous to know' English Romantic poet Lord Byron is born today.

1879
Having invaded Zululand, South Africa, and established a supply camp at Rorke's Drift, British commander Lord Chelmsford moves on to Isandlwana where his entire force is today wiped out in the most humiliating defeat the British Army has yet endured.

1949
Mao Tse-Tung marches into Beijing to mark the beginning of the Communist Regime in China.

1950
Former advisor to President Franklin D. Roosevelt, Alger Hiss is today found guilty of perjury by the commission exploring the possibility of his being a Soviet agent.

1970
The first 'Jumbo' takes off from JFK International in New York to land at Heathrow, London.

23
JANUARY

1849
The British-born Elizabeth Blackwell receives her medical degree from the Geneva College in New York to become the first female doctor in the US.

1920
Wanted for war crimes, the fallen German Kaiser Wilhelm II hides out in the Dutch town of Doorn and when the Allies demand his return, the Dutch Queen Wilhelmina refuses to hand him over.

1960
The French scientist Jacques Piccard, in the company of US Navy Lieutenant Don Walsh, takes the bathyscaphe *Trieste* to the unprecedented depth of 35,800 feet (10,900 m) in the Mariana Trench off the coast of the Philippines.

1989
The extravagant Spanish Catalan surrealist painter Salvador Dalí dies of heart failure.

2004
The Mars Express probe sends back evidence of frozen water at the planet's South Pole.

2013
The US Army lifts the 2004 ban on women serving in combat roles.

41

Roman Emperor Caligula is murdered by his own guard. As a child called Gaius, he liked to hang out with the troops and had his own pair of miniature caliga, the regulation Roman Army footwear, and it was the troops who gave him the nickname of Caligula, or 'Little Boots'.

1616

The Dutch navigator Willem Schouten is the first to round the southern tip of South America. He names the headland in honour of his hometown of Hoorn but the English will mistake this for Cape Horn.

1848

Hired to dig out the foundations for a new sawmill, James Wilson Marshall strikes gold to start the California Gold Rush.

1943

US President Roosevelt and British Prime Minister Churchill conclude their wartime conference in Casablanca where they decide that only unconditional surrender by the Nazis will end the War.

1965

Seventy years to the day after the death of his father, British Prime Minister Winston Churchill himself dies, aged ninety – exactly double his father's age at death.

25
JANUARY

1858

Prince Frederick of Prussia marries the British Princess Victoria, who elects to enter the church to the strains of a piece of incidental music written by Mendelssohn for a production of *A Midsummer Night's Dream*. From this day, it will be known as 'The Wedding March'.

1947

American gangster Al 'Scarface' Capone dies, his power broken in 1931 by an eleven-year sentence for tax evasion.

1955

Russia formally announces the end of hostilities with Germany and a close to their involvement in the Second World War.

1971

Charles Manson is today convicted of the 1969 Sharon Tate murders. Taught to play the guitar in prison in the 1950s by Alvin 'Creepy' Karpis – the last surviving member of the Ma Barker Gang – upon release Manson worked with the Beach Boys before accusing them of stealing his songs and, some say, this started his hatred of celebrities in general.

1983

Madame Chiang Ch'ing (Jiang Qing), the sixty-eight-year-old widow of Chairman Mao, is handed down a suspended death sentence for counter-revolutionary activities.

26
JANUARY

1788
Dismissing Botany Bay as a suitable land for settlement, Governor Arthur Phillip, in charge of the First Fleet transporting convicts to Australia, today decides to move up the coast to Port Jackson and establish what will become Sydney.

1828
The popularity of the Duke of Wellington, after his defeat of Napoleon Bonaparte of France, sweeps him into office as Britain's prime minister.

1905
On his routine morning inspection of the Premier Mine outside Pretoria, South Africa, Captain Frederick Wells notices a glint in the wall of the digs and prises out the Cullinan Diamond, weighing approximately one-and-a-third pounds (600 g).

1934
Advertised as being 'full of ordinary speak and write language', the Shanghai Correctly English Society publishes its *Correctly English in Hundred Days*.

1972
A Yugoslavian airliner is torn apart by a bomb while flying over the Czech Republic. Flight attendant Vesna Vulović survives her fall of over 33,330 feet (10,160 m), the highest fall without a parachute ever recorded.

27
JANUARY

1343
Pope Clement VI sanctions the selling of indulgences whereby a person can buy a pardon for sins committed. Eventually, indulgences will allegedly be sold to cover sins not yet committed, becoming a major concern for Martin Luther and leading to the founding of the Protestant Church.

1825
The American Congress votes to move all Native Americans out of their south-eastern homelands and force them into an Indian Territory in what is now Oklahoma. This will be forever remembered by the tribes involved as The Trail of Tears on which over 4,000 Cherokee alone died.

1967
American astronauts Gus Grissom, Ed White and Roger Chaffee die of smoke inhalation from a flash-fire while testing the systems aboard their Apollo I as it stands on the launch pad at Cape Kennedy (Cape Canaveral).

1973
The Peace Accords, ending US military involvement in Vietnam, are signed in Paris

1987
Mikhail Gorbachev unveils his policy of Glasnost, or Openness.

28
JANUARY

1887

A freak snowstorm hits United States Army post, Fort Keogh, Montana, dropping the largest snowflakes on record, the largest found measuring 15 inches (38 cm) wide and 8 inches (20 cm) thick.

1932

Japanese troops march into Shanghai to start their full-scale invasion of China.

1933

While living in Cambridge, Muslim Nationalist Choudhry Rahmat Ali coins the name Pakistan for his new homeland. Not only does 'pak' mean pure in Urdu but it embraces the provinces of the Punjab, Afghania, Kashmir, Sindh and Baluchistan.

1935

Iceland becomes the first country to legalize abortion.

1986

After five aborted launch attempts, the *Challenger Shuttle* lifts off only to explode seconds later when its fuel tanks rupture. All are killed, including social studies teacher Christa McAuliffe who had won her seat on board in a national competition. Her death puts a stop to the Teacher in Space programme.

29
JANUARY

1596
English sea captain and privateer Sir Francis Drake is buried at sea off the coast of Panama after he dies of dysentery.

1886
Karl Benz reveals the first petrol-powered vehicle. Powered by the newly designed four-stroke engine of Nikolaus Otto, it is an open two-seater on three wheels.

1920
Walt Disney gets his first job as a commercial artist earning $40 a week with the Kansas City Slide Company. Mickey Mouse was the creation of his early partner, Ub Iwerks; Disney never quite managed to draw the character.

1929
Having studied the methods of German dog-training institutions created to help blind veterans of the First World War, the first Seeing Eye Dog School opens in New Jersey.

1944
Otherwise known as The Mighty Mo, USS *Missouri* is launched today as the last battleship commissioned by the United States.

1978
Sweden becomes the first country to ban aerosol sprays due to their alleged effect on the ozone layer.

30

1649

King Charles I of England is executed. Oliver Cromwell, leader of the Parliamentarians who opposed the monarchy, was among those who signed his death warrant.

1933

Adolf Hitler is appointed Chancellor of Germany.

1945

Clearly marked as a hospital ship, the German liner *Wilhelm Gustloff* is sunk by the Allies off Danzig with the loss of around 10,000 civilians; that is six-fold the death toll of the *Titanic* and the greatest single loss at sea.

1948

Mahatma Gandhi is assassinated by Hindu extremist Nathuram Godse.

1972

In Londonderry, Northern Ireland, British troops, claiming to have come under fire from Catholic protesters mounting an illegal march, return fire, killing thirteen immediately in what will become known as Bloody Sunday.

1973

Former aides of US President Nixon, G. Gordon Liddy and James McCord, are convicted of spying on the Democratic headquarters in the Watergate building.

31
JANUARY

1606

Guido (Guy) Fawkes, found guilty of the Gunpowder Plot to assassinate the Protestant English king, is today drawn, hanged and quartered – not hanged, drawn and quartered as the sentence is popularly rendered. This barbaric practice, not abolished until 1870, condemned the guilty to be *drawn* in a dung-cart to a place of lawful execution, *hanged*, but not until dead, and then taken down and cut into *quarters* while still alive.

1858

After numerous delays, British engineer Isambard Kingdom Brunel launches his final project, an iron sailing steamship SS *Great Eastern*, at Millwall, London.

1950

US President Harry Truman gives the go-ahead for the development of the hydrogen bomb.

1985

South African President Botha offers to free Nelson Mandela, leader of the banned African National Congress, if he promises to renounce 'violence as a political weapon'. Mandela rejects the offer.

2001

A Scottish court sitting in the Netherlands today hands down a twenty-year sentence to Abdelbaset al-Megrahi for the bombing of Pan Am Flight 103 over Lockerbie, Scotland, in 1988.

1

1908

King Carlos I and his son, Prince Luís, are killed in Lisbon by some of their own soldiers as the opening gambit of a doomed republican coup in Portugal.

1924

The British Labour Government proclaims its recognition of the Bolshevik Government of Russia.

1942

The German Occupation forces in Norway install Vidkun Quisling as a puppet prime minister. After the War, he is killed by firing squad but his name lives on as an epithet for any traitor.

1978

An escaped slave who helped organize the Underground Railroad before working as a Union spy in the Civil War, Harriet Tubman becomes the first African-American woman to be honoured on an American stamp.

1979

The Ayatollah Khomeini flies home in triumph to replace the Shah of Iran who, with his family and their plundered millions, has already fled to Egypt before moving on to other ports of sanctuary.

2003

The US Space Shuttle Columbia disintegrates on re-entry, killing all seven crew members.

2
FEBRUARY

1665

An English fleet captures the Dutch colony of New Amsterdam in the New World and renames it New York, not after the English city but in honour of the Duke of York, later King James II.

1848

The end of the Mexican-American War, with America acquiring Texas, California, Nevada, Utah, most of New Mexico and Arizona, and parts of Colorado and Wyoming.

1901

The state funeral of Britain's Queen Victoria. Horses bedecked to pull the gun-carriage become unmanageable so Naval ratings take up the harness, thus setting the style for all subsequent state funerals.

1977

The controversial Pompidou Centre opens to the public in Paris.

1986

Somewhat belatedly, the tiny state of Liechtenstein grants women the vote.

1990

In a landmark speech to the parliament in Cape Town, President F.W. de Klerk announces the end of Apartheid, the lifting of the ban on the ANC and the impending freedom of Nelson Mandela.

1448

The Portuguese explorer Bartolomeu Dias is the first European to land on African soil when he puts ashore on the Eastern Cape.

1637

The bubble finally bursts on the Netherlands' 'Tulipomania' as thousands of speculators are left penniless after paying a fortune for tulip bulbs.

1954

Elizabeth II becomes the first reigning British monarch of Australia to visit Australia.

1960

Harold Macmillan makes his famous 'Winds of Change' speech in the South African Parliament, telling the assembly that the days of their Apartheid Regime are numbered.

1971

New York policeman Frank Serpico is set up by fellow officers to be shot during a phoney drugs bust. He famously survives to blow the whistle on wholesale corruption within his own department.

1989

After thirty-five years of draconian rule, General Stroessner is ousted from power in Paraguay. An avid Nazi himself, he has harboured more German war criminals than any other South American dictator.

4
FEBRUARY

1846
The first Mormons depart from Nauvoo in Illinois, the gathering-point for the trek westwards to the new Mormon settlement of Salt Lake City, Utah, under leader Brigham Young.

1911
Rolls-Royce commission their iconic Spirit of Ecstasy statuette from sculptor Charles Sykes. His scantily clad model will be Eleanor Thornton, the secretary and mistress of Lord Montagu of Beaulieu.

1948
Taking its independence of the UK, the nation of Sri Lanka rejects the imposed British colonial name of Ceylon in 1972.

1987
Having successfully sued the British *Daily Mirror* for £8,000 in 1959 for insinuating he was gay, American pianist and vocalist Liberace dies of an AIDS-related illness.

2003
Yugoslavia is today formally dissolved and resurrected as Serbia and Montenegro.

2006
Outraged Syrians burn down the Danish and Norwegian Embassies in Damascus, Syria, after cartoons of Mohammed as a blood-crazed terrorist are printed in Danish newspapers.

5
FEBRUARY

1597

The increasing number of Christian converts are viewed with suspicion in Japan so today twenty-six are crucified in Nagasaki. Each is raised on a cross and then pierced with spears. Many more martyrs are to follow.

1782

England loses control of Minorca when it is today recaptured by the Spanish.

1958

Having first seen the light of day in America in 1935, the parking meter makes its debut in London's Mayfair.

1971

Apollo 14 astronauts Shepard and Mitchell land their module on the Moon where they will remain for the next thirty-three hours.

1976

The swine flu epidemic begins in Fort Dix, New Jersey. On this day, Private David Lewis falls ill at his barracks and becomes the first to die of the infection.

1997

The Swiss banks collectively announce a fund of £71 million to be made available to survivors of the Holocaust. It is estimated that over $400 million was looted from the Jews and put into Swiss bank vaults.

6
FEBRUARY

1778
Revolutionary France becomes the first state to offer official recognition to the government of the newly independent America.

1918
In Britain, the vote is granted to women over the age of thirty if either they, or their husband, own property.

1938
A series of freak waves strike Australia's Bondi Beach. Five people are dragged from the beach and drowned while more than 250 others have to be rescued by boat after being taken over a mile out to sea.

1943
Frank Sinatra makes his singing debut on a popular American radio show, on the same day that Hollywood actor Errol Flynn is cleared of the rape of two teenage girls.

1952
The death of Britain's King George VI occasions the demise of the Crown to his daughter Elizabeth II.

1958
Seven Manchester United footballers are among the twenty-three killed when their plane skids and crashes on the runway at Munich Airport.

7

FEBRUARY

1301

Prince Edward of England, later Edward II, is invested at Caernarfon Castle as the First Prince of Wales in a move to pacify the cross-border fighting between the English and Welsh.

1886

While digging out the footings for his new cottage, Australian miner George Harrison hits the main gold-bearing reef of the Witwatersrand under what is now Johannesburg.

1971

Lagging behind much of Europe, Switzerland finally allows women the right to vote and to hold official positions.

1984

American astronauts Bruce McCandless and Robert Stewart exit their shuttle without safety lines to test the new rocket-powered Manned Manoeuvering Units. The first men to free-manoeuvre in space, the photographs they take of each other are now iconic.

1986

The corrupt President 'Baby Doc' Duvalier flees the wrath of the Haitian people the day before they rise up against him.

1995

Ramzi Yousef, the mastermind behind the 1993 lorry-bombing of the World Trade Center, New York City, is arrested in Islamabad, Pakistan.

8
FEBRUARY

1587

Mary Stuart, aka Mary, Queen of Scots, is today beheaded after being found guilty of conspiring to assassinate Elizabeth I.

1692

Mary Walcott, Abigail Williams, Betty Parris and others feign fits and fake visions to get over fifty people locked up for witchcraft, leading to the execution of twenty of them by hanging or crushing in Salem, Massachusetts, USA. None of the accused were burned at the stake.

1725

Catherine the Great of Russia, born of humble origins, takes the throne, the first woman to rule Imperial Russia.

1924

Chinese Tong gang murderer Gee Jon becomes the first to die in a gas chamber. At first, officials had tried pumping cyanide gas straight into his cell as he slept but the gas escaped through the bars and convinced them they needed an airtight chamber.

1983

Criminals kidnap Shergar from his stable in County Kildare, Ireland, and demand a £5 million ransom. The multiple owners, including business magnate the Aga Khan do not pay the ransom and the most valued racehorse in the world is never recovered.

9
FEBRUARY

1801

The Treaty of Lunéville is signed today to bring peace between the French Republic and the Holy Roman Empire.

1942

During conversion to a troopship, SS *Normandie* is gutted by fire in New York, allegedly on the orders of the incarcerated mob boss 'Lucky' Luciano who wants to convince the authorities that German saboteurs are active in the docklands.

1943

The last Japanese troops evacuate Guadalcanal, now part of the Solomon Islands, giving Allied forces a clear victory in their first major Second World War offensive against Japan.

1972

British Prime Minister Edward Heath declares a State of Emergency today as the Miners' Strike enters its second month; he also establishes formal diplomatic relations with East Germany.

1981

General Jaruzelski takes over in Poland today, promising to crack down on Lech Walesa's Solidarity Movement, the Soviet bloc's first independent trade union.

1996

The Irish Republican Army ends the seventeen-month ceasefire by bombing London's Docklands.

1763

After defeat in the Seven Years' War, France abandons all claim to Canada and acknowledges British sovereignty of the entire country.

1840

Queen Victoria marries her first cousin, Prince Albert.

1913

Captain Scott and his last remaining companions die of starvation, a mere eleven miles from food and safety.

1942

Band leader Glenn Miller is today presented with a solid gold pressing of his hit *Chattanooga Choo-Choo*, the first record to sell one million copies.

1955

Black residents are displaced to shacks where they have no land rights after South African police illegally evict 60,000 from their homes in Sophiatown, outside Johannesburg, and bulldoze the entire township.

1996

IBM's supercomputer Deep Blue plays against Grand Chess Master Garry Kasparov; in their second match, Deep Blue becomes the first computer to defeat a world chess champion.

11
FEBRUARY

1858

The daughter of a miller of Lourdes in France claims to have encountered the Virgin Mary, who demands that she build a shrine to her in the grottos at nearby Massabielle. Now the shrine at Lourdes attracts more than 5 million pilgrims a year.

1929

Italy's Prime Minister Benito Mussolini signs the Lateran Treaty to give the Vatican City the status of an independent state.

1975

Margaret Thatcher becomes the first female leader of the Conservative Party, and in 1979 will become the first female prime minister in the UK.

1990

Nelson Mandela finally walks to freedom after twenty-seven years spent either doing hard labour or confined in his tiny cell.

2006

US Vice President Dick Cheney is on a quail hunt in Texas when, turning to fire at a bird rising behind him, he shoots the seventy-eight-year-old lawyer, Harry Whittington, lodging shotgun pellets in the man's face, neck and chest.

2012

Megastar Whitney Houston is found dead in Suite 434 of the Beverly Hilton Hotel.

12

FEBRUARY

1554

Hailed Queen for Nine Days, Protestant Lady Jane Grey is executed, aged just sixteen, on the orders of her Catholic cousin, Mary Tudor, who then takes the English throne.

1881

Prima ballerina Anna Pavlova is born today in Russia and becomes known for her signature dance, 'The Dying Swan'.

1908

The New York–Paris auto race starts today. Drivers have to head west to Alaska, thence to Siberia and then across all of Europe. There are only six entrants – three French cars, one Italian, one German and one American – with George Schuster of the latter the winner.

1946

African-American US Army Sergeant and decorated War veteran Isaac Woodard is dragged off his bus in Batesville, South Carolina, and blinded by the local Police Chief, Linwood Shull, who pokes him in the eyes with the end of his nightstick. Shull is never prosecuted but the incident gains a momentum none could have imagined.

2004

The Mattel Toy Company announces that Ken and Barbie are splitting up as San Francisco issues the first permits for same-sex marriages.

13
FEBRUARY

1689

With English King James II having fled to France, the last
vestiges of Catholic control are swept away as the Dutch
William of Orange and his wife Mary ascend the English
throne by invitation. To mark the event, a new strain of orange
carrot is bred to replace the more traditional purple varieties.

1917

Exotic dancer Mata Hari is today arrested as a German spy by
the French Army. Shot by firing squad later the same year, her
embalmed head will be stored in the Paris Museum of Anatomy
until 1954 when it is stolen.

1935

Bruno Hauptmann is convicted for the kidnapping and murder
of American aviator Charles Lindbergh's baby.

1960

The French conduct their first atomic test in the Sahara.

1969

The first human eggs are successfully fertilized in a test tube at
Cambridge University by Patrick Steptoe and his team.

2002

Former Yugoslav President Slobodan Milošević goes on trial for
genocide and assorted war crimes committed throughout the
Balkans War.

14
FEBRUARY

1875

American inventor Alexander Bell files his patent application for a telephone the same day that Elisha Gray files an application for a similar device. Gray withdraws his application and Bell is granted the patent, though with much controversy over who should receive credit for the invention.

1918

More than 400 years behind parts of Europe, Russia finally adopts the Gregorian calendar; uniformity will not be achieved until Greece follows suit in 1923 and Turkey, the last, in 1927.

1944

Allied bombers unload over Dresden, Germany, starting a firestorm that destroys the city centre. The city is packed with refugees fleeing the advancing Russian Army and many thousands are killed. With people reduced to ash, no one can be sure of the actual death toll.

1989

Ornithologist James Bond, an expert on Caribbean birds, dies today aged 89. Writer Ian Fleming, a keen bird-watcher living in Jamaica, took his name for his fictional hero and sent Bond a copy of his first book endorsed, 'To the real James Bond – from the thief of his identity.' That book will be auctioned in 2008 for £56,000.

1898

Sent to Cuba to protect US citizens during the Cuban revolt against Spain, the battleship USS *Maine* is blown up in Havana Harbour, leading to the Spanish-American War soon after.

1933

US President Franklin D. Roosevelt is visiting Miami when the mentally unbalanced Giuseppe Zangara tries to shoot him. Fortunately for Roosevelt, the five-foot-tall Zangara has to stand on a rickety chair which collapses when he starts firing, causing him to hit and kill Anton Cermak, Mayor of Chicago, instead.

1942

Singapore falls to Japanese troops who have sneaked up on bicycles from inland and attacked en-masse.

2003

An estimated 600 cities around the world host demonstrations against the war in Iraq today. Estimated to involve 30 million people, it is the largest demonstration the world has ever seen.

2013

At about 9:20 am local time, a meteor in shallow descent explodes over Chelyabinsk in Russia. The number of injured is high with many receiving eye-damage from the blast which produces a flash thirty times brighter than the sun and with between twenty and thirty times more energy than was released from the atomic bomb detonated at Hiroshima.

16
FEBRUARY

1646

With the Royalist defeat at the Battle of Torrington in Devon, the English Civil War is effectively over.

1801

British Prime Minister Pitt the Younger resigns today after 'mad' King George III rejects his recommendation for the emancipation of Irish Catholics.

1881

The Canadian Pacific Railway is incorporated by Act of Parliament at Ottawa.

1968

The 911 emergency service is trialled in the American state of Alabama, and pronounced a success.

1983

More than 8,000 people are evacuated from their homes as bushfires blaze out of control in one of Australia's costliest natural disasters. Within twelve hours, 2,500 are left homeless and 75 people and 350,000 livestock will have lost their lives.

1985

The political group Hezbollah, or The Party of God, is founded in Lebanon.

17
FEBRUARY

1621

English military officer Myles Standish is elected as the First Commander of the New World Plymouth Colony.

1753

In Sweden, today is followed by 1st March as the country makes the transition from the old Julian Calendar to the new Gregorian format and the necessary adjustment of dropping eleven days.

1838

Exasperated by incursions into their territories, the Zulus attack several Dutch camps and settlements in what will become KwaZulu-Natal, South Africa, killing around 500 Dutch emigrants near the settlement of Weenen.

1933

The Blaine Act is passed as the first step in the abolition of Prohibition in America.

1940

In the last recorded use of the cutlass by any Royal Navy boarding-party, the crew of the British HMS *Cossack* swing across in fine pirate style to the German prison-ship *Altmark* in Jøssingfjord, Norway, to effect the release of 299 British prisoners.

18
FEBRUARY

1911

The first airmail flight takes off in India to transport 6,000 letters from Allahabad to Naini Junction.

1930

To prove livestock could be transported unharmed by air, Nellie Jay, hereafter known as The Flying Cow, is airlifted today and milked en route to the International Air Exposition in St Louis in the US. Once over the city, the milk is parachuted down to host Charles Lindbergh who drinks a glass and pronounces it fine.

1949

John Haigh, aka The Acid Bath Killer, murders his last victim, Mrs Olive Durand-Deacon, and dissolves her body, thereby missing out on a fortune. He had feigned interest in her business idea for artificial acrylic fashion fingernails to lure her to her death, little realizing that the lady was about ten years ahead of the market and that they would have made a killing together.

He will be executed in August on six counts of murder.

2008

Cuban leader Fidel Castro announces he will not stand for re-election and a few days later his brother Raúl is voted President. Fidel, now eighty-one, has survived numerous bizarre assassination attempts by the Americans, who have attempted to substitute his cigars with exploding ones, spray him with thallium to make his beard fall out, and salt the seabed at his favourite diving spot with explosive shells.

19
FEBRUARY

1861

Tsar Alexander II offers freedom to more than 20 million Russians enslaved by the medieval serf system. But to gain their freedom they must pay a redemption tax to the government, which is so high many serfs have to sell all their grain to pay it.

1878

American inventor Thomas Edison today takes out a patent on the phonograph, the first record player that can both record and reproduce sounds.

1915

Turkish fortification along the Dardanelles comes under attack by a Franco-British fleet trying to reopen the Black Sea access to Russia, which is desperate for war supplies.

1942

A task force of 242 Japanese planes bomb Darwin in Australia. This is the first and the largest such attack on the country with around 1,000 killed or wounded and several ships sunk in the harbour.

1945

The first of 70,000 American troops lands today on the Japanese island of Iwo Jima to face a smaller but determined and well-dug-in Japanese force. In one of the bloodiest battles in Marine Corps history, the Americans will secure the island with nearly 7,000 marines dead and 20,000 wounded.

20
FEBRUARY

1938

British Foreign Secretary, Anthony Eden, resigns in protest at Prime Minister Neville Chamberlain's decision to talk with Benito Mussolini when Mussolini was violating another agreement.

1947

Appointed Viceroy of India, Lord Louis Mountbatten begins the disentanglement of British rule of that country, which will be abandoned to a Muslim-Hindu civil war of unbelievable savagery from both sides.

1958

The British Government announces the closure of the Navy Dockyards at Sheerness, south-east England.

1985

Contraceptives go on sale in the Republic of Ireland for the first time in the face of stiff resistance from the Catholic Church.

1986

The Soviets launch the Mir Space Station.

2013

Estonia becomes the first country to establish a national network for the fast recharging of electric cars.

21
FEBRUARY

1848

The Communist Manifesto is published today with joint authorship in Karl Marx and Friedrich Engels.

1958

Artist Gerald Holtom today unveils his internationally recognized Peace/CND sign. A conscientious objector throughout the Second World War, Holtom's design is inspired by the semaphore flag-stance for the letters 'N' and 'D', as in nuclear disarmament.

1965

In favour of segregation and not integration, African-American Muslim minister and human rights activist Malcolm Little, aka Malcolm X, is assassinated in mid-speech by rival members of the Nation of Islam at the Audubon Ballroom in New York.

1989

Two of Winnie Mandela's so-called Mandela United Football Club, Mrs Mandela's personal bodyguards, are arrested for the murder of the fourteen-year-old Stompie Moeketsi, suspected of being an informant.

1991

English ballerina Margot Fonteyn dies in Panama City. In 1955 she had married diplomat Roberto Arias and helped him in an alleged coup to bring down the Panamanian government, which failed at the last minute.

22
FEBRUARY

1797

The last invasion of mainland Britain occurs with 1,500 troops from Revolutionary France landing at Fishguard, Wales, hoping to rouse the Welsh against the English.

1879

American merchant Frank W. Woolworth opens up his first 'five-cent' store in Utica, New York.

1897

Charles Blondin dies today. This is the man who walked across Niagara Falls on a tightrope, pushing a stove in a wheelbarrow so he could pause in the middle to cook an omelette for lunch.

1940

The five-year-old Tenzin Gyatso is today enthroned in Lhasa, Tibet, as the 14th Dalai Lama.

1997

The existence of Dolly the Sheep is announced today by the Roslin Institute in Edinburgh, Scotland. Explaining the name of this first cloned animal, Dr Ian Wilmut revealed that Dolly Parton came to his mind as he was taking the cloning cells from a mammary gland.

2011

The Christchurch earthquake strikes today, just before 1 pm, killing 185 people and shattering the town.

23
FEBRUARY

1820

The Cato Street Conspiracy is blown by an undercover policeman who has infiltrated the group. Led by London estate agent Arthur Thistlewood, the group was about to plant a bomb in Grosvenor Square to eliminate the Cabinet as it sat for dinner.

1887

An unrepeated phenomenon, the French Riviera is hit by a massive earthquake that kills over 2,000.

1931

The lady who inspired Escoffier to create both melba toast and Peach Melba, Nellie Melba dies today. Born Helen 'Nellie' Mitchell, the singer took her stage name from the city of Melbourne where she was born.

1945

At about 10:30 this morning, five US marines from Easy Company struggle under enemy fire to raise the American flag on a makeshift pole on top of Mount Suribachi, Iwo Jima. Associated Press photographer Joe Rosenthal snapped the event and the result is now world-famous.

2014

Concert pianist Alice Herz-Sommer, the oldest known survivor of the Holocaust, dies today in London aged 110. She counted the likes of Franz Kafka and Gustav Mahler as family friends.

24
FEBRUARY

303
The persecution of Christians in Rome gets official sanction today from Emperor Galerius.

1525
The Holy Roman Emperor Charles V's troops beat the French in the decisive Battle of Pavia.

1848
France announces the Second Republic as King Louis Philippe flees to sanctuary in Britain.

1917
British Foreign Minister Arthur Balfour is today shown the deciphered Zimmermann Telegram as sent by the German Minister of Foreign Affairs, Arthur Zimmermann, to the Mexican Government. The telegram promises the return to Mexico of Texas, Arizona and New Mexico if Mexico joins the German war effort against the United States.

1920
The National Socialist German Workers' Party publishes its plan for the establishment of the Third Reich.

1988
Mark, the first baby conceived with a frozen embryo, is delivered by caesarean section to Ann Forrester at London's Dulwich Hospital.

25
FEBRUARY

1570

Branding her a usurper, Pope Pius V excommunicates English Protestant Queen Elizabeth I for the execution of Catholic Mary, Queen of Scots.

1850

English surgeon and social reformer Dr William Penny Brookes organizes the first revival of the Greek Olympics in the Shropshire village of Much Wenlock. The Guest of Honour at the 1890 Games will be the French Baron de Coubertin who will take the idea and begin the international modern Olympics in Athens in 1896.

1862

In an effort to conserve metal for the American Civil War and to generate much-needed funds, the Union prints the first-ever 'greenbacks' – paper dollars.

1945

Having stood neutral until the final stages of the Second World War, Turkey declares war on both Japan and Germany to place itself on the winning side without firing a shot.

1978

Still married in name to Lord Snowdon, Princess Margaret shocks the world by openly travelling with lover Roddy Llewellyn to their romantic tryst on Martinique.

26
FEBRUARY

1815
Napoleon escapes from his captors on Elba and returns to France.

1901
The leaders of the failed Boxer Rebellion are today executed in China. The group against foreigners in China is known as the I-ho Ch'uan, or 'Righteous and Harmonious Fists'. Westerners brand the rebels 'The Boxers'.

1935
Robert Watson-Watt demonstrates the first radar equipment at Daventry in Britain.

1991
Kuwait City is liberated after 208 days of Iraqi occupation. This effectively ends the Gulf War, in which the Coalition Forces sustain 190 deaths from Iraqi fire out of a total of around 400 – the exact death toll of Iraqi forces and civilians is unknown but estimated at more than 100,000.

1993
Presaging the horrors that are to come, a massive car bomb explodes in the car park under the World Trade Center in New York, killing six people. Rather prophetically, stockbroker and eyewitness to the blast Bruce Pomper says on the news that it felt like a plane had hit the building.

1827

Although Mardi Gras – translated as Greasy Tuesday – has been celebrated in New Orleans for some time, today sees the first Mardi Gras parade.

1864

The first Union POWs of the American Civil War arrive at the notorious Andersonville Prison in Georgia. Some distance in from the main walls are the Dead Lines and any prisoner stepping over these will be presumed attempting escape and shot. It was the post-war trial of the camp's commander, Henry Wirz, that put the term into general use for the final date of anything.

1939

France and Britain declare recognition of General Franco's regime in Spain.

1948

After forcing President Beneš to resign, the Czechoslovakian Communist Party seizes power in Prague and declares affiliation to Soviet Russia.

2013

Pope Benedict XVI makes his farewell address to the Vatican. With all others dying in office, he is the first pope to resign since Gregory XII in 1415.

28
FEBRUARY

1874

English-born Arthur Orton is today sentenced to fourteen years in prison for fraud. The portly butcher from Australia had presented himself as Sir Roger Tichborne who was lost at sea in 1853. Having gained early support in his fraud, Orton was finally unmasked and his folly parodied in the music hall act of the diminutive Harry Relph, aka Little Tich, hence the term 'titchy' that is now used for anything small.

1973

Two hundred Native American activists occupying Wounded Knee on the Pine Ridge Reservation in South Dakota and the US Military become entrenched today during a seventy-one day occupation of this site of Indian massacres perpetrated by the US Army in 1890.

1975

In the height of the morning rush hour, a London Underground train accelerates into the buffers at Moorgate Station and hits the wall at full speed. It will take three days to get everybody out, with a death toll of more than forty.

1986

With security never having been an issue, Swedish Prime Minister Olof Palme is shot dead as he leaves a Stockholm cinema with his wife, Lisbet, who is also injured in the attack. The apparently motive-less crime remains unsolved.

29
FEBRUARY

1288

Today Scotland enshrines in law the tradition of Leap Year Day marriage proposals from women to men. Any man refusing the offer of marriage will now be required to pay financial compensation to the rejected party.

1940

For her portrayal of Mammy in *Gone with the Wind*, Hattie McDaniel becomes the first African-American actor to win an Oscar. But, at the awards ceremony, she and her escort are not allowed to sit with the other cast members and are put instead on a segregated table.

1960

Amid a storm of protest from women's groups, Hugh Hefner opens the first Playboy Club in Chicago.

1972

In a co-ordinated Franco-American operation that mirrors the plot of *The French Connection* (1971), the Corsican drugs trade is crippled when 415 kilos (915 lbs) of heroin is seized on a fishing boat as it sails out of Marseilles for Miami.

1988

South African Archbishop Desmond Tutu and other clergymen are arrested today as they rally outside the Cape Town Parliament Building in protest at the death sentence imposed on the Sharpeville Six.

1
MARCH

1555

French pharmacist Nostradamus publishes the first of his allegedly prophetic quatrains – rhymed four-line verses about impending disasters. He gives no dates and his writing is open to interpretation.

1815

Having escaped his exile in Elba, Napoleon lands in the South of France with a small but rapidly growing army to have another go at world domination.

1880

Pennsylvania becomes the first American state to outlaw slavery.

1940

The previously unknown British actress Vivien Leigh picks up an Oscar for her role as Scarlett O'Hara in *Gone with the Wind*.

1950

German-born physicist Klaus Fuchs is stripped of his British citizenship and sentenced to fourteen years in prison for feeding data from the British atomic bomb project to his Soviet handlers.

1954

The US detonates a 15-megaton atomic bomb on Bikini Atoll in the Pacific. After the first test there in 1946, French fashion designers marketed the two-piece swimming costume of the same name.

2

1836
Demanding freedom from oppression, Texas proclaims independence from Mexico.

1917
In the face of increasing hostility from the Russian population and open disobedience from his Army, Tsar Nicholas II abdicates today.

1917
Through the power of the Jones Act, all Puerto Ricans may now have US citizenship.

1949
The first non-stop round-the-world flight ends today when American Captain James Gallagher lands at Fort Worth in Texas where he and his fourteen-man crew took off ninety-four hours ago in Lucky Lady II, which had to be refuelled in mid-air four times.

1986
British Queen Elizabeth II signs the Australia Act in Canberra to sever all constitutional ties between Britain and Australia.

2004
The exploratory vehicle Mars Rover reports back to earth that there is evidence that liquid water once flowed on Mars.

3
MARCH

1789

American Major General Nathanael Greene and his troops cross the Yadkin River in a strategic retreat from British Army Officer Cornwallis. Greene will go on to liberate southern American states from British control.

1924

In the first steps to bring Turkey into the modern era, new Turkish President Kemal Atatürk abolishes the Caliphate and disestablishes Islam from the State.

1931

American President Herbert Hoover announces that Congress has passed the resolution to make 'The Star Spangled Banner' the national anthem. The lyrics, written by Francis Scott Key during the War of 1812 with Britain, were set to the favourite drinking song of the Anacreontic Society, a London gentlemen's club.

1974

A Turkish DC10 plane crashes into the Ermenonville Forest, north of Paris, killing all 346 on board.

1985

The Miners' Strike finally ends in Britain today after delegates vote by a narrow margin – 98 to 91 – to return a year after it began. Marked by extreme violence by both the police and the strikers, this was one of the worst industrial disputes in UK history.

4
MARCH

1681

English King Charles II grants Royal Charter to the Quaker William Penn to colonize the New World and found Pennsylvania. The name comes from the Penn surname and sylvania, Latin for 'forest land'.

1790

In the largest exercise of gerrymandering in history, Revolutionary France divides itself into eighty-three departments to destroy the rise of regionalism and fragment the power of the major landowners.

1966

English musician John Lennon today proclaims, in an interview with London's *Evening Standard*, that The Beatles are more popular than Jesus Christ. In America there are spontaneous demonstrations with disillusioned fans burning their record collections in public.

1989

Pope John Paul II denounces *The Satanic Verses* as blasphemous due to its implication that sections of the Koran are inspired by the Devil. British author Salman Rushdie is forced into hiding when he receives death threats, including a *fatwā* issued by Iranian Leader Ayatollah Khomeini.

5
MARCH

1770

An angry mob gathers outside the Customs House in Boston, Massachusetts, and British troops fire on the crowd, killing five. Branded 'The Boston Massacre', American propagandists claim this a case of troops gunning down peaceful citizens but Revolutionary leader John Adams successfully defends the soldiers in court.

1930

American entrepreneur Clarence Birdseye launches eighteen lines of frozen food in stores in Springfield, Massachusetts. Travelling in Labrador in Canada he had noted how the Inuits would catch fish and speed-freeze it in the air. This rapidity of freeze was the key element that led to Birdseye's success.

1946

Speaking in the American city of Fulton, Missouri, British politician and wartime prime minister, Churchill, makes reference to an Iron Curtain that has descended to bisect Europe.

1953

Bank-robber-turned-revolutionary Joseph Stalin dies, ostensibly of a brain haemorrhage. Conspiracy theories suggest it is more likely due to the administration of the rat poison warfarin.

6
MARCH

1836

The Mexican Army launches an assault on the Alamo Mission after a thirteen-day siege. The defending Texas settlers perish, but within two months the colonists will succeed in establishing the Republic of Texas. In some reports, a handful of Texans are taken prisoner and then executed, including Davy Crockett, who will become an American folk hero.

1869

Russian chemist Dmitri Mendeleev presents his first draft of the Periodic Table to the Russian Chemical Society.

1899

A 'new' wonder-drug is today launched by the German pharmaceutical company, Bayer. Trademarked Aspirin, the active ingredient is acetylsalicylic acid, which is present in the bark of the willow tree, as chewed in Ancient Rome to relieve pain.

1951

Americans Ethel and Julius Rosenberg stand trial for passing atomic secrets to the Soviets. Such spies normally got long prison terms so there is a national intake of breath when they are given the death sentence.

1960

The United States today announces it is sending 3,500 troops into Vietnam.

7
MARCH

1912

The French aviator Henri Seimet becomes the first to fly non-stop from Paris to London.

1936

Adolf Hitler takes his first step towards war when, in contravention of the Versailles Treaty and the Locarno Pact, he marches his troops into the Rhineland.

1945

Exactly nine years to the day after Hitler invaded the Rhineland, Allied troops cross the bridge at Remagen to enter the same territory, pushing German resistance back to Berlin.

1965

Protesting the murder of the unarmed African-American civil rights protestor Jimmie Lee Jackson, shot by police for interfering in their whipping of his mother and eighty-two-year-old grandfather, a march is organized from Selma to the Alabama State Capitol of Montgomery. Hundreds are left bleeding after police wade in with tear gas and nightsticks.

1989

Tired of Tibet's pleas for independence and the reinstatement of the exiled Dalai Lama, Beijing sends in troops to contain riots and imposes martial law. Foreigners are deported. The Dalai Lama will make known his concerns about the use of violence under martial law.

8
MARCH

1702

The unpopular William III of England dies of injuries sustained falling off his horse after it tripped on a molehill in Hampton Court gardens.

1817

The New York Stock Exchange opens its offices on Wall Street, so named because it ran along the line of the early stockade built to keep out the Native Americans.

1917

In a Russia on the brink of revolution, today is the first day that the tsar's soldiers refuse to fire on the crowds, many of them opting instead to join the mob.

1949

'Axis Sally', an all-American broadcaster from Maine, USA, is sent to prison for treason. Stranded in Berlin at the outbreak of the Second World War, she had worked for the Germans throughout the War, making taunting broadcasts intended to demoralize American troops fighting in Europe.

1989

Long associated with Mafia money-laundering and other nefarious activities, Archbishop Paul Marcinkus resigns control of the Vatican Bank. Marcinkus said that 'you can't run the Church on Hail Marys'.

9

MARCH

1796

Future Emperor of the French, Napoleon Bonaparte, marries Joséphine in one of the most infamous love affairs in history. On their wedding night her pug dog, Fortuné, bites Napoleon on the calf. Two days later he leaves to invade Italy.

1831

The French Foreign Legion is founded in Algeria and along with it the myth that fugitives can join up in order to escape the authorities. This image no longer applies as the Legion now conducts thorough background checks on all applicants.

1956

Archbishop of Cyprus Michael Makarios is exiled by British authorities for his part in the nationalist paramilitary organization EOKA, which seeks independence from Britain and a union with Greece. Mikarios will become president of a free Cyprus four years later.

1959

Barbie doll makes her commercial debut at the American Toy Fair in New York City. On a trip to Germany in 1956, Mattel Toy Company owners, Ruth and Elliot Handler, had spotted an adult-figured realistic-looking doll marketed as Bild Lilli, a gag gift for adults. They bought some as presents before bowdlerizing Lilli into Barbie.

10
MARCH

1922

Nationalist leader Gandhi is arrested for sedition in India and sentenced to six years, but released two years later on account of his appendicitis. He will go on to lead India to independence from Britain in 1947.

1952

Pre-empting the forthcoming elections, General Fulgencio Batista mounts a military coup in Cuba and takes sole control. His first job is to open the island up to American mobsters and take his cut of what will become the Latin Las Vegas. He will be a rich man by the time Castro ousts him from power.

1982

Triggering fears of moonquakes, earthquakes and even Armageddon, today sees a celestial syzygy in which all the planets form a line out from the sun. Nothing happened.

1987

The Vatican openly condemns all surrogacy motherhood, artificial insemination and any laboratory interference with the conception process.

1990

Accused of being an Israeli spy working for the British, Iranian-British journalist Farzad Bazoft is sentenced to death on the orders of Saddam Hussein. Despite pleas from world leaders, Bazoft will be executed five days later, to international outrage.

11
MARCH

1845

A poorly translated Treaty of Waitangi, granting sovereignty of New Zealand to Britain, leads to misunderstandings and the First Māori Uprising. Today the Māori attack Kororareka (later Russell) and drive out all the settlers.

1941

Still walking the fine line of neutrality, President Roosevelt announces the Lend-Lease Act whereby he pledges American industrial might to the Allied war effort without his having to commit troops.

1985

Following the death of Konstantin Chernenko, Mikhail Gorbachev is today inaugurated as the youngest Secretary General to have control of the Soviet Union.

2006

Slobodan Milošević, 'The Butcher of the Balkans', dies of a heart attack in his cell during his war crimes trial in The Hague.

2011

An earthquake of about Magnitude 9 in north-eastern Japan triggers the shutdown of circuits at the Fukushima nuclear plant. The cooling system is also compromised, so when the subsequent tsunami destroys the back-up generators the plant starts to leak out radioactive material, causing a widespread evacuation.

12
MARCH

1881
Determined to cement its foothold in North Africa, France forces Tunisia to become a French protectorate.

1913
In Australia, to stop the Sydney-Melbourne argument as to which should be the nation's capital, today sees the founding of a brand new city in rurally situated Canberra. The name is thought to derive from a native term for a meeting place.

1928
Built by William Mulholland of Mulholland Drive fame, the St Francis Dam collapses, sending a two-mile-wide wall of water through Los Angeles County. More than 600 are killed with some of the bodies found as far south as the Mexican border.

1945
A matter of weeks short of her sixteenth birthday, Anne Frank dies of typhus in Bergen-Belsen Concentration Camp.

1993
In a worrying turn of events, North Korea announces its decision to withdraw from the Nuclear Non-proliferation Treaty and says that UN nuclear inspectors will no longer be admitted border access.

1994
The Church of England ordains its first female priests.

13
MARCH

1881

After surviving several other assassination attempts, Tsar Alexander II is finally killed today. The first bomb thrown at his carriage in St Petersburg explodes wide of its target, prompting him to get out and investigate, giving the second bomber a perfect target.

1894

The first professional and full striptease is staged at the Divan Fayonau Music Hall in Paris. Entitled 'Yvette's Bedtime'.

1961

Pablo Picasso, aged seventy-nine, marries his thirty-seven-year-old model and muse, Jacqueline Rocque. He will die in 1973 and she will shoot herself in 1986.

1972

American writer Clifford Irving stands up in court today, admitting his 'authorized biography' of Howard Hughes to be largely fiction. He had hoped that the notoriously reclusive Hughes would not challenge him – he was wrong.

1979

While Grenada's Prime Minister Sir Eric Gairy stuns the United Nations in New York with his demands for a special committee to investigate UFOs, as he himself had recently encountered one, he is ousted from power back home in Grenada in a Marxist coup led by Maurice Bishop.

1489

Queen Catherine Cornaro of Cyprus is forced to abdicate and Cyprus becomes a colony of the Republic of Venice. Throughout her reign the island had been controlled by Venetian merchants.

1883

German revolutionary socialist Karl Marx is interred in Highgate Cemetery.

1932

Having perfected his Kodak camera and the film-processing system, George Eastman commits suicide today leaving a note proclaiming, 'My work is done. Why wait?'

1943

The ethnic cleansing of the Kraków Ghetto, Poland, is completed on the orders of SS Captain Amon Goeth. All Jews are either killed or shipped out to extermination camps. One of the few escapees is ten-year-old Roman Polanski who will grow up to be the troubled film director.

1945

An Avro Lancaster plane from the British 617 Dambuster Squadron drops the heaviest bomb of the War. Designed by Barnes Wallis, the 22,000-pound (9,980-kg) Grand Slam hits the Bielefeld Viaduct in Germany with shock waves destroying more than 100 yards (90 m) of the viaduct.

15
MARCH

44BC

Roman Dictator Julius Caesar is assassinated, not in the Senate but in a meeting room adjacent to the Theatre of Pompey. There is no evidence that he said anything as he lay dying, but in Shakespeare's play *Julius Caesar*, his dying words are 'Et tu, Brute?' ('You too, Brutus?') uttered to his friend Marcus Brutus.

1792

British General Cornwallis is in India to crush the last resistance to the British invasion and today defeats Tipu Sultan, the Tiger of Mysore, who is forced to hand over his two sons as hostages and sign the Treaty of Seringapatam. This signs a large portion of his kingdom over to the East India Company, a powerful trading group owned by British merchants and aristocrats.

1937

The Hungarian Dr Bernard Fantus establishes the world's first refrigerated blood storage facility in the USA, naming it the Cook County Hospital Blood Preservation Department. Fantus's nickname for the unit, the Blood Bank, will soon take over.

1990

Described by President Bush Snr. as 'Brazil's Indiana Jones', Fernando Collor de Mello becomes the first people-elected president that Brazil has had in thirty years. His tenure will end in 1992 on charges of corruption.

16
MARCH

1912

The day before his thirty-second birthday, the incapacitated Lawrence 'Titus' Oates walks out of Captain Scott's tent to his death, during the doomed return journey across the Ross Ice Shelf at the South Pole. Scott recorded in his diary Oates's now famous last words: 'I am just going outside and may be some time'.

1935

Casting aside the terms of the Treaty of Versailles, Hitler introduces Conscription to swell the German Army.

1968

The village of My Lai in Vietnam will today enter the history books after American troops, under the command of Lt William Laws Calley, rape and murder more than 300 men, women and children. After a show trial, President Nixon has Calley's life sentence overturned to leave him serving only three years under house arrest in his own quarters in Fort Benning.

1978

The revolutionary Red Brigade kidnaps former Italian Prime Minister Aldo Moro from his motorcade as it passes along the Via Fani in Rome. As the Administration refuses to make a deal with the kidnappers, Pope Paul VI offers himself in exchange but Moro's bullet-riddled body will be later discovered in the trunk of an old Renault 4.

17
MARCH

1959

The USS *Skate* surfaces at the North Pole after completing its landmark journey under the ice.

1968

The first major UK demonstration against the war in Vietnam takes place outside the American Embassy in London's Grosvenor Square. After actress Vanessa Redgrave is allowed to deliver a petition, things turn ugly as mounted police make repeated charges into the crowds.

1969

Disappointing the ultra-Orthodox elements in Israel, who are bitterly opposed to women being involved in religious or political matters, seventy-year-old grandmother Golda Meir takes her position as its first female prime minister. She was called the Iron Lady long before Britain's Margaret Thatcher.

1978

Carrying over 1.6 million barrels of crude oil, the *Amoco Cadiz* splits in half off the coast of Brittany, France, and spills its cargo into the sea.

1995

English gangland killer Ronnie Kray dies after collapsing with a heart attack at the high-security psychiatric hospital, Broadmoor.

18
MARCH

1241

About as far west as they extend their influence, the Mongol Hordes today sack the Polish City of Kraków before withdrawing a few days later.

1314

Jacques de Molay, the last Grand Master of the Knights Templar, is burned to death in Paris, along with Geoffroi de Charny, the first recorded owner of the Turin Shroud. Both die a slow and agonizing death, as demanded by King Philip IV who is in debt to the Templars.

1890

The inexperienced Kaiser Wilhelm II dismisses Bismarck as German Chancellor.

1965

Soviet cosmonaut Aleksey Leonov takes off in Voskhod 2 to become the first man to walk in space. Leonov spends just over twelve minutes turning somersaults, expanding his suit so much that he is then too 'fat' to get back into the capsule. After playing around with some bleed-valves he makes a safe return.

1978

After a show trial orchestrated by General Zia of Pakistan, the recently deposed Prime Minister Zulfikar Ali Bhutto is sentenced to death; appeals and international pressure ignored, he will be hanged in Rawalpindi jail in April the following year.

19
MARCH

1791

The Constitutional Act is voted through today to establish the two distinct and separate British Colonies of Upper and Lower Canada with equal rights guaranteed for French-speaking settlers. It will be another fifty years before a united Canada comes into being.

1834

The so-called Tolpuddle Martyrs of Dorset in south-west England are today sentenced to transportation for having signed a union agreement demanding better working conditions on the local farms. Using outdated legislation, they are found guilty of taking an illegal oath and sent to Australia for seven years.

1945

The USS *Franklin* is seriously damaged by a kamikaze attack off the Japanese coast. In all, such attacks only sank about forty-seven ships at the cost of around 4,000 planes and pilots.

1945

Hitler issues his so-called Nero Decree, which calls for all buildings of importance in Germany to be destroyed to prevent their use by the Allied forces.

2011

Named after the hot wind that blows out of the Sahara at this time of year, Operation Harmattan sees the invasion of Libya by French forces attacking by land, sea and air.

20
MARCH

1792

The French National Assembly approves the adoption of the guillotine as a more humane method of execution for the poor. Hitherto, only the aristocrats were accorded beheading while the common man had to endure more painful and protracted methods.

1815

Returned from exile in Elba, Napoleon enters Paris in triumph to the consternation of other nations. In response, Britain, Russia, Prussia and Austria make a pact in Vienna to unite against him.

1995

Thirteen die, 54 are seriously injured and 1,000 are hospitalized after members of the Aum Shinrikyo cult release sarin gas in the Tokyo subway.

2003

The US launches a first wave of missiles at Baghdad in Operation Desert Storm, while Saddam Hussein is still promising the world the 'Mother of all Battles'.

2010

Dormant since 1823, the Eyjafjallajökull volcano in Iceland erupts to cause disruption across Europe. As the ash-cloud spreads, air traffic grinds to a halt amid fears of bunged-up jet engines failing under the load. Holidaymakers are left stranded.

21
MARCH

1788

With no fire department in place to stem the rampage of the Great Fire of New Orleans, more than 80 per cent of the colonial city is destroyed.

1829

Despite being sixty years old and the serving prime minister, the Duke of Wellington challenges the Earl of Winchilsea to a duel on Battersea Fields, London, in a row over Catholic Emancipation. When the Duke turns he deliberately fires wide when he sees that his opponent has not raised his own gun; Winchilsea then fires into the ground and British honour is saved.

1871

The Iron Chancellor of Germany, Otto von Bismarck, opens the inaugural parliament of what he proclaims the Second Reich. The First Reich was the so-called Holy Roman Empire, as centred in Germany under Otto the Great.

1960

Protesting the Pass Laws, requiring blacks to carry travel permits at all times, around 20,000 black South Africans march into Sharpeville where they are 'kettled' by armed police and buzzed by low-flying jets. Without warning, police fire Sten guns, killing 70 and injuring 200, the majority of whom are shot in the back as they flee in panic.

1765

The British Government passes the Stamp Act, levying a direct tax on materials printed for commercial use in the American colonies. Unpopular and eventually repealed, the Act will plant the seeds for America's fight for independence from Britain.

1907

Gandhi begins his campaign of Civil Disobedience in South Africa – but he is no opponent of Apartheid. He is a firm supporter of the caste system, and objects to the lumping together of high-caste Indians with natives of Africa.

1933

The Nazis open their first concentration camp at Dachau, ostensibly for the internment of political undesirables. The camp becomes a training centre for SS guards and a model for other concentration camps.

1945

Inspired by the Alexandria Protocol the previous year, the Arab League is formed, uniting all the Arab states in Africa with those in the Middle East.

1997

The Comet Hale-Bopp makes its closest ever pass of planet Earth.

23
MARCH

1775

In opposition to the Stamp Act raised against the American colonies by the British Government, American Revolutionary leader Patrick Henry makes his famous 'Give me liberty or give me death' speech in the Virginia House of Burgesses.

1801

A group of Russian Army officers led by General Zubov force Tsar Paul I to sign abdication papers before strangling and kicking him to death on the floor. Zubov then drags the tsar's twenty-three-year-old son, Alexander, from his bed, telling him, 'Time to grow up. Go and rule.'

1919

Led by one-time communist, Benito Mussolini, a group of disenchanted left-wingers forms the National Fascist Party in Milan.

1925

Tennessee becomes the first US state to outlaw the teaching of Evolution or even the very mention of Charles Darwin's name in a classroom. In a few short months this law will be challenged at the infamous Scopes Trial.

1989

Measuring over 1,000 feet (300 m) in diameter, an asteroid comes within 430,000 miles (690,000 km) of Earth which, in celestial terms, counts as a near miss.

24
MARCH

1839

Chinese troops seize 20,000 chests of opium from British traders in an attempt to stop it flooding the country, an action that will invite the British to attack in the First Opium War.

1911

Denmark abolishes the death sentence.

1944

At least eighty Allied POW's held in Stalag Luft III in eastern Germany escape through their tunnel. Three evade capture but fifty are rounded up and shot by the Gestapo with the rest being returned to camp. The events are the subject of the feature film, *The Great Escape.*

1976

Isabel Perón is ousted from the Presidency of Argentina in a bloodless military coup. The ex-nightclub dancer is the third wife and widow of former President Juan Perón.

1988

Israeli nuclear technician Mordechai Vanunu is sentenced to eighteen years for revealing the existence of the secret Israeli nuclear bomb programme to the British Press. To get him to trial, Mossad agents drugged him in his London hotel and then hustled him onto a ship.

25
MARCH

1306

Crowned at Scone, Scotland's new king is Robert de Brus of Flemish ancestry, but he will forever be known as Robert the Bruce.

1807

William Wilberforce pushes the Slave Trade Act through the British Parliament today to outlaw the trade throughout the Empire. In reality, the Slave Triangle continues unabated with British ships heading for Africa to pick up consignments of slaves who are bartered for tobacco and rum in the New World, which can be sold back in the UK with 'clean hands'.

1931

Nine black youths are arrested in Alabama, south-east USA, for the rape of two white women who have been free-riding in the same freight car. Sentences ranging from seventy-five years to death will be handed down, despite one of the women admitting that she has lied in court and that no one has raped anyone. Known as the Scottsboro Boys, their case will be the subject of countless books and films.

1975

Saudi Arabian King Faisal is shot by his nephew, Prince Faisal, in the Riyadh Palace. The prince is condemned to death on 18 June and taken straight from the court to the public square for beheading.

26
MARCH

1812

The Boston *Sentinel* coins the term 'gerrymander' after Governor Elbridge Gerry of Massachusetts, USA, re-draws county boundaries to maximize the number of favourable voters. Essex County now looks like a salamander so the paper prints a cartoon of the county depicted as such.

1920

The first detachment of the dreaded Black and Tans arrives in Ireland to fight the growing menace of the Irish Republican Army. They are Special Police recruited to assist the Royal Irish Constabulary and so called for the colour of their uniforms.

1942

The first trains arrive at Auschwitz.

1973

Mrs Susan Shaw becomes the first female trader allowed onto the hallowed floor of the London Stock Exchange.

1979

In a landmark meeting arranged and hosted by American President Jimmy Carter, Israel's Menachem Begin and Egypt's President Sadat sign an agreement to restore diplomatic relations.

2000

Vladimir Putin is elected President of Russia, replacing Boris Yeltsin in the Kremlin.

27
MARCH

1814

General (later President) Andrew Jackson helps determine the outcome of the Creek Indian Nation civil war in a massive battle at Horseshoe Bend in Alabama, south-east USA. Around 4,000 Red Stick Creek Indians lose out to a combined force of 7,000 of Jackson's American state militias allied with Lower Creek and Cherokee Indians. The shattered Creek Nation is forced to cede its territory – more than 21 million acres (8.5 million hectares) of Alabama and Georgia – to the US Government.

1968

Celebrity cosmonaut Yuri Gagarin dies in a plane crash outside Moscow. Piloting a MiG-15 training jet, he fails to bring the aircraft out of a spin.

1977

Today sees the worst air disaster in history as two 747s crash into each other at Tenerife Airport. Diverted from Gran Canaria Airport because of a bomb attack, the KLM aircraft attempts to take off while the Pan-Am is on the runway. All 248 KLM passengers and crew die in the fireball with 583 total fatalities.

1981

Poland grinds to a halt under a massive four-hour national warning strike orchestrated by Lech Walesa's Solidarity Movement, forcing the Polish Government to concede to some of the group's demands.

28
MARCH

845

Paris is attacked by Vikings under the control of Ragnar Lodbrok, nicknamed Hairy Breeches, referring to the animal-skin trousers that he wore.

1910

French aviator Henri Fabre takes off at Marseilles in his Fabre Hydravion, the world's first successful sea-plane.

1939

Franco wins the Spanish Civil War with the bloodless capture of Madrid. The city, held by Republican loyalists, had been under siege since 1936 when journalists had asked Nationalist General Mola if his advancing four columns were enough and he famously replied that he had a fifth column already at work inside the city. This allusion to spies and saboteurs enshrined the term 'fifth-columnist' in the English language for such operatives.

1968

Brazilian high school student Edson Souto is shot dead by police during a protest demanding cheaper canteen meals for the less well-off students.

1979

The nuclear reactor at Three Mile Island in Harrisburg, Pennsylvania, goes into partial meltdown; faulty coolant valves are to blame.

29
MARCH

1792
Gustav III, dilettante scientist and King of Sweden, is assassinated. To prove coffee was dangerous he took twins convicted of murder and commuted their sentence to life with the proviso that one drank three pots of tea a day, with the other consuming similar amounts of coffee. Both outlived him.

1852
Ohio in Midwestern US makes it illegal for women or children to work more than a ten-hour day.

1943
Rationing begins in the United States with butter and cheese becoming the first products to be controlled.

1961
Congress ratifies the Twenty-third Amendment, thereby allowing residents of Washington DC to cast votes in presidential elections for the first time in history.

1979
As his army loses ground to Tanzanian troops sent in by neighbouring President Nyerere, Ugandan dictator Idi Amin flees the capital, Kampala. Having murdered as many as 500,000 Ugandans through his brutal regime, Amin will escape justice by finding sanctuary in Saudi Arabia where he will die in 2003.

30
MARCH

1856

Today sees the close of the Crimean War, the last serious engagement the British will fight in their conspicuous red coats. During the conflict, Sir William Russell, viewing the stand of the British troops against Russian cavalry from a distance, stated in his report to *The Times* that they seemed but 'a thin red streak'. This was picked up by the public as 'thin red line' and has been a synonym for military resolve ever since.

1867

The US Secretary of State, William H. Seward, today finalizes the purchase of Alaska from Russia for $7.2 million, which works out to about two cents per acre. Pilloried in the press as Seward's Folly, the true value of the land will not be discovered until the Klondike Gold Strike in 1896.

1903

Residents close to Niagara Falls wake up to an eerie silence as their national attraction has run dry. An ice jam further up the river has completely cut off the flow.

1981

John Hinckley Jr. shoots American President Ronald Reagan as he exits a Washington hotel, in a bizarre bid to win the attention of the actress Jodie Foster. Recovering in hospital, Reagan quips to his wife, Nancy: 'Honey, I forgot to duck', as previously said by boxer Jack Dempsey to his own wife after getting beaten by Gene Tunney.

31
MARCH

1889

Using the techniques he perfected in the infrastructure of the Statue of Liberty, Alexandre Eiffel opens his Paris tower to a mixed reception. Some love it but many Parisians hate it. Designed to be the centrepiece of the Paris Exhibition, there will be moves to have it dismantled after the show is closed.

1896

Austrian businessman Emil Jellinek strikes a deal with Gottlieb Daimler to buy a race car designed to Jellinek's specifications and given the brand name of Mercedes, after Jellinek's eleven-year-old daughter.

1909

The keel of RMS *Titanic* is laid today in Belfast and construction of the ill-fated liner begins.

1950

Norwegian adventurer Thor Heyerdahl publishes a popular English translation of his account of his epic journey across the Pacific on his Kon-Tiki raft made of wood and reeds.

1959

With the Chinese invaders trying to stamp out adherence to the Buddhist faith in Tibet, the Dalai Lama slips quietly out of the country, walking for fifteen days to the foot of the Himalayan Mountains which he then has to cross into India.

1
APRIL

1318

The border town of Berwick-upon-Tweed is wrested from English control by the Scots. This small town changed hands so often that declarations of war on England sometimes specified whether it was included or not. Having been omitted from the Treaty of Paris that closed the Crimean War, the town was still technically at war with Russia until 1966 when a mutual declaration of peace was made between the town's mayor and a Russian representative.

1924

Adolf Hitler is sentenced to five years in prison for his failed Beer Hall Putsch but gets out within a year. In prison he will pen *Mein Kampf*, which will sell over 10 million copies.

1948

After the French, British and Americans announce their intention to unify their sectors of Berlin into West Berlin, the Soviets retaliate today with the imposition of checks on traffic in and out of their own section. The Berlin Wall will follow.

1984

For reasons unclear, the father of American singer Marvin Gaye shoots and kills his son in the family home tonight.

2001

The Netherlands becomes the first country to legalize same-sex marriage.

2
APRIL

1513
Spanish explorers land in the New World on the day of their festival of Pascua Florida, or the Easter of the Flowers, and so name it Florida.

1792
The Coinage Act is passed in America to establish the dollar as the official currency and replace the Spanish piece-of-eight currently in wide circulation.

1979
Vietnamese invaders of Cambodia show the world the first footage of the horrors of Communist Khmer Rouge leader Pol Pot's regime: mountains of skulls and human remains are televised around the world.

1989
Russian leader Mikhail Gorbachev flies into Cuba to try and mend fences with President Fidel Castro after the Soviet climb-down over the Missile Crisis and the subsequent cut in Soviet subsidies for Cuba.

1992
New York Mafia boss John Gotti, aka the Teflon Don, is today handed down life without parole for his many crimes as head of the Gambino Family Syndicate.

3
APRIL

1860

Changing horses every 10 miles (16 km) and expected to cover 80 miles (128 km) a day, the first Pony Express rider sets out from St Joseph in Missouri, USA, with mail for California. As famous as this venture is, the telegraph will put it out of business in less than a year.

1888

Prostitute Emma Smith, argued to be the first victim of London serial killer Jack the Ripper, is attacked and dies of her injuries the next day.

1948

US President Truman today signs the authorization for the Marshall Plan to release billions of dollars to rebuild a war-ravaged Europe.

1968

At the Mason Temple in Memphis, Tennessee, USA, Martin Luther King delivers his landmark 'I've been to the Mountaintop' speech. He is killed the next day.

1973

Motorola showcase the first hand-held mobile phone.

1981

The Osborne 1, the first practicable and portable PC, is unveiled at the West Coast Computer Faire in San Francisco, California, USA.

4
APRIL

1581

Having completed his circumnavigation of the world and returned to England, Francis Drake is knighted by Elizabeth I.

1818

After entertaining several designs, the American Congress finally settles on the agreed design for the US flag as having thirteen stripes and one star for each state of the Union.

1949

Theodore Achilles, grandson of the president of the Eastman Kodak camera company, today presides over the foundation of NATO in Washington. The treaty will eventually be signed by most members of non-Communist Europe and Scandinavia to present a united front to the Warsaw Pact bloc.

1968

At about 6 pm, American Civil Rights activist Martin Luther King is leaning over the balcony of his motel to talk to colleagues below when he is shot dead by sniper James Earl Ray.

1975

With Da Nang fallen and Saigon under heavy artillery fire, the first plane of Operation Babylift is loaded with Vietnamese orphans and cleared for take-off only to be brought down by ground fire. Hearing of the tragedy, American businessman Robert Macauley mortgages his house to charter a Pan-Am 747 to bring out several hundred orphans for adoption in the US.

5
APRIL

1794

French Revolution leader Georges Danton, who was actually middle class, as were many of his compatriots, is sent to the guillotine today. Up to 40,000 people went to the guillotine: 72 per cent were commoners, 14 per cent middle class, 6 per cent clergy and only 8 per cent were aristocrats.

1919

Frenchman Gaston Georges Quien is convicted and condemned to death for his collaboration with the Germans. He betrayed British nurse Edith Cavell and her organization which helped Allied servicemen escape from Occupied France.

1955

Buckingham Palace announces that the eighty-year-old Sir Winston Churchill is to resign as Prime Minister of Britain and will be replaced by Sir Anthony Eden.

1960

Ben-Hur wins an unprecedented eleven Academy Awards at the Oscars. Riddled with historical inaccuracies – the Romans did not, for example, use slave labour in their galleys – the film is based on the 1880 book by Lew Wallace.

1976

Reclusive millionaire Howard Hughes dies in Texas, USA, leaving a $1.5 billion estate.

6
APRIL

1814
Napoleon is forced into unconditional abdication after British, Russian, Prussian and Swedish troops occupy Paris.

1896
Inspired by the revival of the Olympic Games, hosted since 1850 in the English village of Much Wenlock, the French Baron Pierre de Coubertin opens his own grander version in Athens today with fourteen nations competing in forty-three events.

1917
With the German submarines sinking an increasing number of American ships, President Woodrow Wilson signs the resolution to take America into the First World War.

1924
Mussolini sweeps the National Election in Italy, beating the runners-up by more than 4 million votes.

1965
Intelsat 1, the first commercial communications satellite, is launched by America, providing nearly instantaneous telephone and television links between the US and Europe.

1968
Following the murder of Martin Luther King, American cities find themselves in the grip of race riots of such severity that the National Guard is called out and curfews are imposed.

7
APRIL

1652

The Dutch establish the settlement that will become Cape Town.

1827

John Walker, a chemist of Stockton-on-Tees in northern England, markets the first ignitable match.

1832

The last recorded case of wife-selling in England. Joseph Thompson of Carlisle leads his wife, Ann, to market in a halter and starts the bidding at 50 shillings. The lady is eventually bought by one Henry Mears for £1 and a Newfoundland dog.

1906

Mount Vesuvius in the Gulf of Naples, Italy, erupts to wreak devastation on Ottaiano and Naples. Even though the latter is 6 miles (9 km) away, many buildings collapse under the weight of ash deposited on their roofs.

1958

Having set out from Trafalgar Square in London on 4 April, the first Ban-the-Bomb march of some 3,000 people today arrives at the gates of the Atomic Weapons Research Establishment at Aldermaston in Berkshire, where they are joined by another 7,000 demonstrators. Two years later, the march for the same campaign will number up to 100,000.

8
APRIL

1820

Searching for a missing sheep, the Greek farmer Yorgos Kentrotas stumbles across a damaged statue on the island of Milos. Soon identified as a representation of Venus, it is now one of the most iconic works of art in the world.

1953

Kenya African Union leader Jomo Kenyatta is sentenced to seven years' hard labour by the British Colonial Administration in Kenya for his alleged leadership of the Mau Mau, a radical anti-colonial movement. On his release he will become prime minister then president of the independent Kenyan nation.

1986

American actor Clint Eastwood is elected Mayor of Carmel, California; afflicted with a lifelong allergy to horses, he suffered a lot in the making of all those Westerns.

1992

Retired American tennis star Arthur Ashe admits that he contracted AIDS from blood transfusions during recent heart surgery. He will die as a result of that contamination by next February, aged but forty-nine.

2013

Ex-British Prime Minister Margaret Thatcher is found dead in her bedroom at the Ritz London.

9
APRIL

1774

After fighting on the wrong side at the Battle of Culloden, the Scottish Jacobite Simon Fraser, 11th Lord Lovat, becomes the last man in Britain to be beheaded at Tower Hill, London. The last ever beheading with an axe in the UK was that of the Luddite Jeremiah Brandreth of Derby on 7 November 1817.

1865

Union officers commandeer the McLean family home in Appomattox, Virginia, for the surrender of the Confederacy in one of the last battles of the American Civil War.

1940

The German Army invades both Norway and Denmark.

1966

Their first marriage of 1957 declared bigamous under Italian law, film producer Carlo Ponti and actress Sophia Loren marry legally.

1992

Manuel Noriega, ex-Panama Dictator, goes on trial in Miami, Florida, on charges of racketeering and drugs trafficking. He will get a thirty-year sentence.

2003

American tanks roll into Baghdad, Iraq, pausing briefly to help the jubilant mob pull down the statue of Saddam Hussein in the main square with a half-track and tow rope.

10
APRIL

1633

Never seen before in England, the exotic banana goes on sale in London shops.

1815

Mount Tambora in Indonesia erupts and remains active until mid-July, killing some 70,000 people. The atmospheric pollution brings on a two-year-long volcanic winter causing global crop failures and the worst famine of the nineteenth century.

1849

American mechanic Walter Hunt takes out a patent on the safety pin. He invented the device while absent-mindedly twisting a piece of wire and pondering how he could raise the money to get himself out of debt.

1912

RMS *Titanic* slips her Southampton moorings to set out on her ill-fated maiden voyage.

1919

Popular revolutionary hero of the Mexican people Emiliano Zapata dies in a hail of bullets in an ambush organized by forces of Mexican President Venustiano Carranza, who is himself assassinated the following year.

11

1713

Under the Treaty of Utrecht, France cedes Gibraltar and Newfoundland to the British.

1945

American troops liberate the Buchenwald Concentration Camp and are stunned by the horrors they find.

1951

Previously stolen from London's Westminster Abbey by Scottish Nationalists, the Stone of Scone, on which all Scottish kings have been crowned, is found at the altar of Arbroath Abbey in Scotland.

1951

Still popular with the American public, General MacArthur is stripped of his command by US President Truman after publicly advocating the extension of the Korean War into China.

1955

An Air India flight blows up over the South China Sea, killing all passengers. The target was Chinese Premier Zhou Enlai who, tipped off about the Chinese Nationalist plot to kill him, sent a decoy delegation on the flight.

1963

Pope John XXIII issues his *Pacem in Terris*. Translating as Peace on Earth, it is the first papal encyclical that is addressed to all people 'of good will', be they Catholic or not.

12
APRIL

1606
The Union Jack is adopted as the official flag of Great Britain.

1831
The Broughton Suspension Bridge in Salford, Manchester, collapses as troops from the 60th Rifle Corps march across. Despite it being established that corroded chains and bolts were to blame, the event starts the myth that troops must break step when crossing any bridge lest the rhythmic stamping sets up a destructive resonance.

1861
General Pierre G.T. Beauregard starts the American Civil War by firing on the Union Fort Sumter in South Carolina. Captain Abner Doubleday returned ineffective fire before the Fort was surrendered without a single casualty on either side.

1864
American Confederate General Nathan Bedford Forrest captures the Union Fort Pillow in Tennessee with a minimal loss of about twenty men. Despite surrendering, up to 400 of the Union troops are massacred including a large proportion who are black.

1990
A routine UK Customs check on a shipment to Iraq of what appear to be oil pipes are revealed to be the disassembled barrel of a super-gun capable of firing a warhead hundreds of miles.

13

APRIL

1742

Handel's *Messiah* debuts in the unlikely venue of the Great Music Hall on Fishamble Street, Dublin, with proceeds going to support debtors in the local prison.

1796

The first elephant arrives in New York from India and becomes a public attraction. Nicknamed Old Bet, the poor animal is gunned down in the streets of Maine by a farmer objecting to people spending money on spectacle and entertainment.

1912

The Royal Flying Corps is established as part of the British Army; it becomes the Royal Air Force after World War I.

1919

Thousands of Sikhs from villages and towns surrounding the Holy City of Amritsar gather in the city to celebrate Baisakhi. Wrongly fearing insurrection, the draconian British General Dyer orders his men to open fire on the unarmed crowd, killing and wounding more than 3,000 men, women and children.

1970

An oxygen tank explodes on the Apollo 13 mission, preventing the planned moon landing. Despite considerable damage to the vehicle, the crew return safe and sound.

14
APRIL

1865
Prominent American actor John Wilkes Booth shoots President Lincoln in Ford's Theatre. Booth allegedly breaks a leg when he jumps down to the stage to make his escape which, in popular folklore, began a tradition of theatricals wishing such injury on each other on opening nights, though the logical connection with good luck is none too clear.

1903
Dr Harry Plotz of New York comes up with a reliable typhus vaccine.

1931
Unpopular Spanish monarch Alfonso XIII flees his homeland in fear of his life after the Republicans win landslide victories in the municipal elections.

1935
Colorado, Wyoming, Kansas and Oklahoma – dubbed the Dust Bowl by the American Press – are hit by the first violent prairie winds that envelop the whole area in a choking dust storm.

1971
President Nixon calls an end to the American blockade against China.

15
APRIL

1755
Dr Samuel Johnson publishes his *Dictionary of the English Language*.

1912
The 'unsinkable' RMS *Titanic* proves everyone wrong after hitting an iceberg, with only 710 of the 2,227 passengers on board surviving; the shortage of lifeboats contributes to the heavy loss.

1927
The first day of the Great Mississippi Flood with New Orleans under 4 feet (1.2 m) of water.

1929
Author Sir James Barrie hands over the royalty rights from *Peter Pan* to the Great Ormond Street Hospital for Sick Children.

1989
Ninety-six people are crushed to death at the Hillsborough football ground in Sheffield, England, with the police cover-up yet to be unravelled.

2013
Two Chechen brothers, Tamerlan and Dzhokhar Tsarnaev, target the finishing line of the Patriots' Day Boston Marathon with bombs made out of old pressure cookers. Three people are killed and another 264 need treatment for shrapnel and blast injuries.

16
APRIL

1746

Dreams of glory are today smashed for the Italian-born Bonnie Prince Charlie, fighting for the Jacobite cause, at the Battle of Culloden in Scotland; he escapes to France in defeat.

1850

Marie Grosholtz dies today. Arrested during the French Revolution, along with her friend Joséphine de Beauharnais who later married Napoleon, she escaped the guillotine after offering to make wax death-masks of those less fortunate. She later married a chap called Tussaud and took her new-found skills to London.

1917

Exiled from Russia and told about the Revolution by his neighbours in Zurich, Lenin allegedly fails to raise the train fare home. Anxious to see the collapse of the tsarist regime and the withdrawal of Russia from the First World War, Germany provides a private train, safe passage to Russia and a reported $10 million spending money to help fund his mission.

1943

While researching the ergot fungus at the Santoz laboratories in Basel, Albert Hofmann accidentally synthesizes LSD and inadvertently ingests a tiny amount. Three days later he takes even more and goes on his famous six-hour technicolor bicycle ride round the city before coming down and enlightening the rest of the world.

17
APRIL

1521

The German monk Martin Luther appears before the Diet of Worms in Germany to defend his ninety-five points of criticism of the Vatican.

1790

American statesman and scientist Benjamin Franklin dies today.

1897

The first UFO hoax occurs today. Residents of Aurora in Texas claim that an alien airship crashed in the town and that the alien pilot was given a Christian burial. The hoax was later acknowledged by one of the pranksters.

1961

Backed by America's CIA, a force of anti-Castro Cubans lands at the Bay of Pigs on the south coast of Cuba in their disastrous invasion. President Kennedy had promised air support but it never materializes and the invaders are all killed or captured.

1986

Israeli security staff at London's Heathrow Airport discover 3.3 pounds (1.5 kg) of Semtex in the baggage of the pregnant Irish woman Anne-Marie Murphy alongside a calculator that is believed to be a time-trigger device for the bomb. Her bags had been packed by her Jordanian boyfriend, Nezar Hindawi, who is swiftly arrested and sentenced to forty-five years in prison, the longest fixed term in British history.

18
APRIL

1775

Paul Revere sets out from Charlestown for Lexington to warn the American Revolutionaries of the British advance.

1906

Early in the morning, San Francisco, USA, is hit by a massive earthquake and subsequent fires devastate the city, killing more than 5,000 and leaving 300,000 homeless. Many seek refuge in the Golden Gate Park where they watch the city burn through the night.

1949

The twenty-six counties of the Irish Free State unite to become the Republic of Ireland.

1956

A Soviet cruiser docks today in Portsmouth, UK, carrying Russian politician Nikita Khrushchev on a diplomatic visit. The next night, celebrity-diver Lionel 'Buster' Crabb, sent into the harbour by MI6 to have a look round the hull, disappears. His headless and handless body will later be found floating in Chichester Harbour.

1968

American tycoon Robert McCulloch buys London Bridge at auction. He will ship it home in kit-form to rebuild it at his self-made Lake Havasu City in Arizona. It is a complete myth that he thought he was buying the more iconic Tower Bridge.

19
APRIL

1689
Famously portrayed by actress Greta Garbo in the 1933 film, Queen Christina of Sweden dies in exile in Rome. She had abdicated in 1654 before heading for Rome dressed as a man.

1775
The first confrontation of the American Revolution as the British Army's infantry, nicknamed Redcoats, exchange fire with militiamen on Lexington Green.

1882
The Father of Evolution, English naturalist Charles Darwin dies today making a widow of his cousin, Emma Wedgwood, of the pottery family. He was an unworldly twenty-two-year-old when he sailed on HMS *Beagle*, not as the expedition's naturalist but as travelling companion to the depressed Captain FitzRoy.

1995
On the second anniversary of the Waco Siege in Texas, USA, the Federal Bureau of Alcohol, Tobacco and Firearms in Oklahoma City is shattered by a massive truck-bomb parked outside. The death toll hits 168. Timothy McVeigh, a Gulf War veteran disgruntled by the Waco affair, is soon detained and will die by lethal injection on 11 June 2001.

1999
The German parliament takes up office again in the renovated Reichstag after it had fallen into disuse following a fire in 1933.

20
APRIL

1657

In America, one of the few Western countries never to have entertained persecution of the Jews, freedom of religion is expressly extended to Jews settling in New Amsterdam (later called New York).

1770

British navigator Captain James Cook logs his first sighting of the Australian mainland, becoming the first European to reach Australia's east coast.

1939

Inspired by the 1930 lynching of African-Americans Thomas Shipp and Abram Smith in Marion, Indiana, American singer-songwriter Billie Holiday today records the first Civil Rights protest song, 'Strange Fruit'.

2010

Leased to British multinational company BP (formerly British Petroleum), the oil-drilling rig *Deepwater Horizon* explodes, killing eleven workers and causing the worst oil spill in history as 170 million gallons of oil leak out before the flow is capped in early June. As all involved play the blame game, the fatal impact on marine and coastal wildlife in the Gulf of Mexico escalates and the final clean-up cost will be in the billions.

21
APRIL

1509

Henry VIII takes the English throne. Far from the bluff character of cinematic romps, Henry ruled by fear and executed at will, the number of people executed during his reign allegedly reaching 72,000.

1836

The Texan Army under Sam Houston crushes the Mexican Army at the battle of San Jacinto in the Texas Revolution. According to legend, the battle commences while Mexican General Santa Anna is busy in his tent with Emily West, a lady of mixed race and said to have a 'high-yellow' complexion. West becomes 'The Yellow Rose of Texas' celebrated in the popular folk song.

1898

Following the sabotage of the battleship USS *Maine* in Havana harbour, America declares war on Spain.

1918

German fighter pilot Manfred von Richthofen, otherwise known as the Red Baron, is killed by ground-fire from Australian Sgt Cedric Popkin and his Vickers machine gun.

1989

Ignoring instructions to disband, more than 100,000 students rally in Beijing's Tiananmen Square. The next day will see the first riots and lootings with unrest persisting until martial law is declared and the tanks roll in.

22

APRIL

1500

Explorer and navigator Pedro Cabral claims Brazil for Portugal. In 1494 Pope Alexander VI, aka Rodrigo Borgia, had tired of Spain and Portugal fighting over new lands so he drew an arbitrary line down the map, calling it the Demarcation Line, ordering each to stick to their respective sides. That is why the rest of South America speaks Spanish.

1889

By noon today, some 50,000 people are lined up for the famous Oklahoma Land Rush. Nearly 2 million acres (809,000 hectares) of the Indian Territory have been thrown open to settlement on a first-come basis. As the land-grab had been announced the previous month, the more pragmatic settlers, branded Sooners, were already in the Territory, with claims neatly staked out.

1915

Poisonous gas for warfare developed by German chemist Fritz Haber is used at the Second Battle of Ypres in France during the First World War. Haber returns home to celebrate, but his wife, seeing his work as a perversion of science, commits suicide. Undeterred, Haber will go on to develop a more effective gas to be used on the Eastern Front in 1916.

1971

Dreaded dictator of Haiti, Papa Doc Duvalier dies today, leaving his collection of severed heads of political rivals to his son and heir, Baby Doc.

23
APRIL

1348

English King Edward III institutes the Order of the Garter, a prestigious honour awarded by the British sovereign to worthy recipients. Its legendary origin was a garter, symbolizing witchcraft, that slipped from the leg of the Countess of Salisbury; uttering the immortal 'Honi soit qui mal y pense', or 'Shamed be the person who thinks evil of this', King Edward put the garter on his own leg, thereby placing himself between the countess and any accusations of coven involvement.

1616

Celebrated English poet and playwright William Shakespeare dies on his fifty-second birthday after a night out with fellow playwright and poet Ben Jonson.

1942

Exeter is bombed during the Second World War in the first of the so-called Baedeker Raids made by the German air force. Using the tourist guide *Baedeker's Great Britain*, by Karl Baedeker, the Germans announced their intention to bomb every building marked with three stars in the guide.

1969

Claiming to have acted to highlight the plight of the Palestinians, Jordanian Sirhan Bishara Sirhan is sentenced to die in the gas chamber for his assassination of US Senator Robert Kennedy. The sentence was later commuted to life.

24
APRIL

1858

After the first attempt cracked under the chiming hammer during tests, the second version of the Great Bell is declared fit for use. Cast on 10 April with a lighter hammer, the Great Bell will be installed in St Stephen's Tower in London in October. The presiding Commissioner of Works is Sir Benjamin Hall, hence the nickname of Big Ben.

1916

The Easter Rising in Dublin sees more than 2,000 Irish paramilitaries seeking Irish independence in Dublin trying to take control of key buildings across the city. The response is met by 16,000 British troops with armoured vehicles.

1980

Humiliation for US President Carter as Operation Eagle Claw spirals into calamity. Sent in to rescue the fifty-two embassy staff held hostage in Iran, most of the helicopters are downed in dust storms and one crashes into a Galaxy transporter. With eight dead the mission is abandoned and Carter will lose out to Reagan in the next election.

2005

Pope Benedict XVI celebrates his inaugural Mass following the death of Pope John Paul II. Unusually for a pope, Joseph Ratzinger had been a member of the Hitler Youth and an anti-aircraft gunner in the German Army.

25
APRIL

1792

Rouget de Lisle pens a jaunty ditty called 'War Song for the Army of the Rhine'. Sung by 500 volunteers from Marseilles as they enter Paris during the French Revolution it is renamed 'La Marseillaise'. With its ability to rouse a mob, the song is repeatedly banned before being adopted as the French National Anthem.

1915

Allied troops land on the Gallipoli Peninsula under harsh fire from the Turkish defenders. Antipodean troops play a significant role in the campaign and the day becomes known as 'Anzac Day', commemorating Australian and New Zealand military losses.

1953

Molecular biologists Francis Crick and James Watson today unveil their model of the double-helix DNA strand.

1966

The old quarters of Tashkent, Uzbekistan, once a trading point on the Old Silk Road, are completely destroyed by an earthquake.

1990

The Hubble Telescope is launched from the space shuttle *Discovery*.

2003

The Human Genome Project, an international programme to map the genes of human beings, is completed today almost three years ahead of schedule.

26
APRIL

1900

Seismologist Charles Richter is born in Ohio, USA. Using a seismograph instrument, he measured the magnitude of earthquakes in terms of the power released within the earth, rather than the surface impact on buildings and people. The Richter Scale was superseded by the Moment Magnitude Scale in 1979.

1937

Spanish Dictator Franco with Nazi German air support bombs Guernica, the old Basque capital in northern Spain, during the Spanish Civil War. The bombers target bridges, railways and arms factories. Correspondents with the Nationalist forces will claim that evidence of aerial bombing in the town was greatly overshadowed by that of sabotage and arson; the Republicans had done the damage themselves.

1964

In East Africa, Tanganyika and Zanzibar merge to form Tanzania.

1986

The reactor at Chernobyl goes into overload, creating a radioactive cloud that will reach as far afield as Scandinavia and the UK.

2008

Austrian Josef Fritzl is arrested after it is discovered he kept his own daughter, Elisabeth, in the cellar of the family home for twenty-four years.

27
APRIL

1521

Determined to convert all the inhabitants of his newly discovered Philippines to Christianity, Portuguese explorer Ferdinand Magellan lands on Mactan where his ministry is not well received. Ordering his crossbowmen to fire on the islanders, he is himself killed in the ensuing melee.

1773

The British Parliament passes the Tea Act, which hits the pockets of colonial tea importers and avaricious tea smugglers and gives the East India Company a virtual monopoly on the tea trade. John Hancock and other Revolutionaries will protest 'no taxation without representation' in the Boston Tea Party later the same year.

1950

The British Government announces recognition of the newly formed State of Israel.

1968

The Abortion Act comes into force today in the UK allowing terminations up to twenty-eight weeks' gestation.

1994

The first all-enfranchised and free elections take place in South Africa to bring majority rule in with a landslide.

28
APRIL

1770

British navigator Captain James Cook drops anchor in Stingray Bay, which he will rename Botany Bay for the variety of plant-life he finds.

1789

The mutiny on board HMS *Bounty* begins under the hand of master's mate Fletcher Christian. Dumping the much-maligned Captain Bligh and eighteen loyal men into an open boat, the mutineers turn tail for the sexual pleasures they have left behind in Tahiti. An extraordinary sailor, Bligh, equipped with a quadrant and pocket watch, takes the boat 3,618 nautical miles (6,701 km) to safe harbour in Timor in the Dutch East Indies.

1887

The world's first car race is held in Paris over a 1.2 mile (2 km) course. Sponsored by a Monsieur Fossier, it is won by Georges Bouton of the De Dion-Bouton Company but, as he is the only contestant who has turned up, this is no surprise.

1945

Having been captured by Partisans, Italian leader Benito Mussolini and his mistress Clara Petacci are shot and the next day hung up on butcher's hooks from the canopy of an Esso petrol station in Milan in northern Italy.

1952

The American Occupation of Japan officially ends.

29
APRIL

1852

In an attempt to distract himself from his depression, Dr Peter Mark Roget publishes his famous thesaurus, a compendium of English words grouped according to their similar or linked meanings.

1885

Oxford University, the oldest university in the English-speaking world, announces that women will be able to sit the institution's entrance examination for the first time.

1930

The first direct telephone link is established between Britain and Australia.

1935

Invented and patented the year before by Percy Shaw, the first cats' eyes are installed. Shaw allegedly got the idea and name from the reflection of a real cat's eyes in his headlights that stopped him crashing off the road in fog as he drove home from his local pub.

1980

English film director Alfred Hitchcock dies aged eighty in Los Angeles, USA. For all his pioneering work in the suspense and psychological thriller genres, he never won an Oscar.

2011

Prince William, eldest son of the heir to the British throne, marries Kate Middleton at Westminster Abbey in London.

30
APRIL

1789

George Washington is inaugurated at the White House as the first President of the United States.

1888

The deadliest hailstorm in history is unleashed over the town of Moradabad in India. Stones the size of grapefruits kill 250 people and countless animals.

1900

Immortalized in song and film, American folk hero and train driver Casey Jones is killed when his legendary Chicago-to-New Orleans Cannonball Express hits a stalled freight train outside Vaughan in Mississippi.

1945

Adolf Hitler commits suicide in his bunker by gunshot, along with wife Eva Braun who ingests cyanide. In accordance with his wishes, their bodies are taken outside and burned.

1993

Yugoslavian tennis-ace Monica Seles is stabbed in the back as she plays Magdalena Maleeva in Hamburg. She is leading 6-4, 4-3 when Günter Parche, a demented fan of Steffi Graf, jumps onto the court and attacks her with a boning knife.

1
MAY

1707

The Acts of Union come into full effect today, joining the fortunes of Scotland and England.

1840

The Penny Black adhesive postage stamp goes on sale in London in readiness for the Penny Post, a new postal system due to open for business in five days' time.

1851

Queen Victoria opens the first World Fair at the purpose-built Crystal Palace in London's Hyde Park. The Fair also provides the first public lavatories with an entry fee of one penny, hence 'going to spend a penny'.

1931

US President Hoover hits a button on his desk in Washington DC to turn on the lights of the Empire State Building in New York for the Grand Opening. A magnet for suicide-jumpers, on 2 December 1979 Elvita Adams will jump from the eighty-sixth floor only to be caught by a freak wind flinging her back through a window on the eighty-fifth and leaving her with a broken hip.

1999

The frozen body of English mountaineer George Mallory is found on Everest, having last been seen alive less than 1,000 feet (305 m) from the summit in 1924.

2
MAY

1936

Only days before the city falls to invading Italians, Abyssinian Emperor Haile Selassie and his family flee Addis Ababa in Ethiopia for the more peaceful environs of Bath in the UK. Backed by British troops he will return to Ethiopia in 1941.

1945

After prolonged street fighting, the Russians announce that they have taken Berlin in what is the final major offensive of the Second World War.

1957

US Senator Joe McCarthy, the leader of so many Communist witch hunts, dies today, aged forty-eight.

1982

The Argentinean cruiser *General Belgrano* is sunk by the British during the Falklands War despite being outside the British-declared Exclusion Zone. Around 320 crewmen perish.

2008

Cyclone Nargis (Urdu for 'daffodil') makes landfall at Myanmar (Burma), killing 140,000 and wreaking more than $4 billion of damage.

2011

American forces finally find and kill Osama bin Laden who is living in Abbottabad in Pakistan.

3
MAY

1494

Genoese navigator Christopher Columbus lands in Jamaica on his second voyage of exploration sponsored by Ferdinand II and Isabella I of Spain. Despite his status in the United States, he never made it to the North American mainland, only to assorted islands in the Caribbean and to Venezuela, South America.

1917

The first American fleet arrives in Britain today to bolster the Royal Navy against the Germans.

1986

Shortly after boarding, Tamil Tiger terrorists detonate a bomb on an Air Lanka plane while grounded at Colombo Airport in Sri Lanka, killing twenty-one.

1989

Born as George, ex-marine Christine Jorgensen dies today having shocked America as the country's first sex-change candidate back in 1952.

2007

Three-year-old English child Madeleine McCann is tonight abducted from the family's holiday accommodation in Portugal, so starting the longest and most highly publicized child-hunt in history.

4
MAY

1904

Motoring and aviation pioneer Charles Rolls and engineer Henry Royce meet in the Midland Hotel in Manchester, England, to sign an agreement to partner up in the car business.

1970

After three days of rioting on Kent State University Campus in Ohio, USA, the National Guard opens fire on students protesting at American involvement in Cambodia. Leaving four dead and nine wounded, similar shootings will occur eleven days later at Jackson State University in Mississippi.

1972

The hitherto unknown Canadian 'Don't Make a Wave' Committee changes its name to the Greenpeace Foundation.

1982

HMS *Sheffield* is hit by a French-made Exocet missile fired by an Argentinean fighter plane during the Falklands War. Oddly enough, the missile failed to detonate but, by fluke, it severed the seawater fire main, leaving the ship to burn out of control and sink a few days later.

1994

The Israeli Prime Minister Yitzhak Rabin and Yasser Arafat of the Palestine Liberation Organization sign an accord today, granting self-rule to the Gaza Strip and Jericho.

5
MAY

1821

While in exile on the island of Saint Helena, Napoleon Bonaparte dies from cancer although rumours spread of possible poisoning by arsenic.

1945

The first day of the uprising in German-occupied Prague at the end of the Second World War. With the Americans and Russians in full advance, Czech resistance snipers pick off German SS troops or lure them into bomb traps. The Germans will wrest back control only to surrender a day later on the arrival of the Russian Red Army.

1980

Today sees the SAS, part of the British Special Forces, storming the Iranian Embassy in London to release the twenty-six hostages being held by gunmen demanding Arab sovereignty of a province in Iran. It is all over in minutes with five of the six terrorists killed.

2010

The first day of public demonstrations and riots at the austerity measures imposed in a Greece teetering on the brink of bankruptcy.

6
MAY

1626

The most famous land deal in history is struck when a Dutch settler in the New World, Peter Minuit, buys Manhattan Island from Native Americans for $24-worth of assorted goods.

1937

With the cause of the fire to be argued for decades, the Hindenburg passenger airship, 'the pride of Germany', explodes in a fireball on docking at Lakehurst Airfield in New Jersey, USA. More than thirty perish.

1954

The British medical student, Roger Bannister, becomes the first man to run a mile in under four minutes.

1974

West German Chancellor, Willy Brandt, resigns after revelations that a member of his personal staff is an East German spy.

1994

English Queen Elizabeth II and French President Mitterrand preside over the opening of the Channel Tunnel rail link between Folkestone and northern France.

7

1763

Tired of the intrusion into their lands, the American Indians of the Odawa tribe declare open war on the British settlers and today begin a five-month siege of the fort in the settlement that will become the town of Detroit in Michigan, USA.

1832

Greece declares its independence from Turkey under the protection of Britain, France and Russia.

1915

Off the south coast of Ireland, Captain Walther Schwieger of the German U-20 fires his first torpedo at British ocean liner RMS *Lusitania*, taking the lives of 1,198 passengers and crew. The sinking caused an international outcry but the ship was not the innocent passenger ship of British propaganda, as it was carrying war munitions and passing through a declared war zone.

1945

The German Chief-of-Staff, General Alfred Jodl, meets with his Allied counterparts at 2:30 am in a small schoolhouse in Rheims, France. At 2:40 am he signs instruments of unconditional surrender and the war in Europe is over.

1975

US President Ford today announces the official end of the Vietnam War.

8
MAY

1429

A French army led by Jeanne d'Arc, or 'Joan of Arc', breaks the English siege of Orléans during the Hundred Years' War, setting in motion the ousting of the English from French soil.

1876

After a life marked by rape and bouts of slavery, Truganini, the last full-blood Aboriginal Tasmanian, dies today aged sixty-four.

1902

With the highly active Mount Pelée rumbling for days, more than 30,000 people crowd into the imagined safety of Saint-Pierre, the main city of the Caribbean island of Martinique, an overseas region of France. But the eruption produces a blast of red-hot gas that hits the town killing everyone in its path, except Auguste Cyparis, who is locked up in an underground cell.

1921

Years ahead of much of Europe, Sweden abolishes the death penalty.

1955

The first scarred survivors of Hiroshima and Nagasaki arrive in America for plastic surgery.

9
MAY

1949

The first launderette opens on London's Queensway with hundreds to follow. Launderettes and the advent of affordable domestic washing machines soon ruin the Chinese laundry industry, their owners turning to other business ventures, including Chinese restaurants.

1972

Black September Palestinian terrorists have taken over Sabena Flight 571 at Tel Aviv Airport and today the rescue begins. Posing as technicians and fuel operatives, a squad of sixteen Israeli commandos, which includes two future Israeli prime ministers, Benjamin Netanyahu and Ehud Barak, storm the plane and release the hostages.

1999

Co-ordinated demonstrations are held in cities across China in protest at yesterday's bombing of the Chinese Embassy in Belgrade by NATO planes embroiled in the Yugoslavian war. Mistaking the building for a Yugoslav military target, US planes had dropped five guided bombs on the embassy, killing four Chinese reporters.

10

MAY

1857

Sepoys mutiny in the ancient Indian city of Meerut, killing their British officers before marching on Delhi. The Hindu and Muslim troops have been alienated through low pay, racial bigotry and, finally, a newly issued batch of ammunition greased with a mixture of cow and pig fat that requires the user to bite off the tip (hence 'to bite the bullet', meaning get ready for action).

1863

Leading American Civil War General of the Confederacy, Thomas 'Stonewall' Jackson, dies of wounds given by his own men. Returning to camp at Chancellorsville in Virginia on the night of 2 May, sentries fired on Jackson and his men believing them to be Union cavalry.

1893

The Supreme Court of the United States of America today finally rules on the matter as to whether a tomato is a fruit or a vegetable, calling them vegetables in order to tax them. Tomatoes are now officially recognized as fruit.

1940

As Hitler's troops march into Holland and Belgium, British Prime Minister Neville Chamberlain is replaced by Winston Churchill who vows to fight, promising the British public nothing but 'blood, toil, tears and sweat'.

11
MAY

1811

Chang and Eng, the original Siamese twins, are born in Siam (now Thailand) and will eventually settle in North Carolina, USA, to marry the Yates sisters, Sarah and Adelaide. They will have twenty-one children between them though the methodology used will never be explained.

1812

The only British prime minister to be assassinated, Spencer Perceval is gunned down in the House of Commons by a malcontent bankrupt called John Bellingham.

1887

Buffalo Bill's Wild West Show is brought to London as part of the celebration of Victoria's Golden Jubilee.

1949

Siam announces it has changed its name to Thailand.

1996

The worst fatalities occur on Mount Everest with a party of eight dying today after being caught in a blizzard.

1998

India raises tensions with neighbouring Pakistan and attracts sanctions from the USA and Japan by detonating three thermo-nuclear devices at the Pokhran Underground Test Site.

12
MAY

1712

John Bull, the personification of England, sees the light of day in a pamphlet published by Scotsman John Arbuthnot.

1861

The Flag Raising Ceremony at Fort Warren near Boston is conducted to the first-ever playing of 'John Brown's Body', aka 'The Battle Hymn of the Republic'. Popularly believed to be a reference to the famous Abolitionist John Brown, the namesake for the song was actually John Brown of Boston, a Sergeant at Fort Warren.

1935

Alcoholics Anonymous is founded by fallen Wall Street trader William Wilson in Ohio, USA.

1949

After nearly a year of unnecessary embargos, Russia lifts its blockade of Berlin and the first food-convoys are allowed into East Germany from the West.

1969

The UK lowers the voting age from twenty-one to eighteen.

2002

Former President Jimmy Carter arrives in Cuba for a five-day visit, making him the first American politician of any standing to extend a hand to President Castro since he took power.

13
MAY

1607

The famous Pilgrim Fathers arrived in America in 1620, but today sees the landing of the first English settlers of Virginia in the New World. Their leader is John Smith, whose life is supposedly saved by Pocahontas (originally named Matoaka), a ten-year-old Indian girl.

1844

In response to outbreaks of civil unrest, Spain forms a national Military Police called the Guardia Civil.

1846

America declares war on Mexico. The Mexican Army carries the British muskets that were gathered up after Waterloo but the Americans have the new revolutionary Colt revolvers and superior cannons and mortars, making their victory inevitable.

1861

Queen Victoria announces Britain's neutrality in all matters relating to the American Civil War.

1958

The French armed forces based in Algeria back a coup to gain independence from Paris during the Algerian Revolution. As they take over key positions in the country, General de Gaulle is called out of retirement and although he finds a resolution this time, the rebellion will reoccur in 1961.

14
MAY

1610

A Catholic zealot called Ravaillac stabs the French King Henry IV as his carriage passes the market of Les Halles in Paris. In the prescribed punishment of the day, Ravaillac is slowly torn apart by four horses.

1796

Decades behind the original pioneers of the procedure, English scientist Edward Jenner conducts his first inoculation against smallpox using the son of his gardener, eight-year-old James Phipps, as his subject. Jenner's success will lead to widespread use of the smallpox vaccine.

1900

The second meeting of the Modern Olympics opens in Paris today, allowing women to compete for the first time.

1948

With the British Mandate in Palestine still running and already in conflict with every surrounding Arab state, David Ben-Gurion declares the establishment of the Zionist State of Israel.

1955

Under the guiding hand of Moscow, Eastern Bloc countries sign up to the Warsaw Pact to present a response to the formation of NATO (North Atlantic Treaty Organization).

15
MAY

1718

London lawyer James Puckle demonstrates the world's first machine guns capable of firing sixty-three rounds in seven minutes. The first model, intended for use against a Christian foe, fires round bullets and the second model, intended for Muslim Turks, fires more damaging square ones.

1928

With planes and pilots supplied by Qantas, the Rev. John Flynn of the Presbyterian Church launches the Australian Inland Mission Aerial Medical Service, which is soon known as the Flying Doctors.

1972

Vehement racist and segregationist Governor George Wallace of Alabama, USA, is touring Maryland when twenty-one-year-old Arthur Bremer calls out to him before opening fire, putting Wallace in a wheelchair for the rest of his life.

1988

The Soviet Army begins its humiliating evacuation from Afghanistan.

1989

As the Chinese military struggle to contain the protests in Tiananmen Square, Mikhail Gorbachev shakes hands with Deng Xiaoping in the Great Hall of the People to signify a rapprochement of the two main Communist nations.

16
MAY

1918

The Sedition Act is passed in America making criticism of the government or war effort an imprisonable offence. The government tries to keep the Act in place after the close of the First World War but Civil Liberty riots enact a change in the law.

1920

Pope Benedict XV today canonizes Joan of Arc, who was burned at the stake as a heretic in 1431.

1943

Known as the 'Dam Busters', 617 Squadron takes off from RAF Scampton, near Lincoln, England, to deliver Barnes Wallis' bouncing bombs to the dams on the Ruhr. Wallis got the idea from reading about Admiral Nelson's technique of cannon skip-shot which, a bit like skimming stones on a lake, was used to put a hole in enemy ships as near to the waterline as possible.

1997

President Mobutu, seen as the archetypal African dictator, escapes Zaire for Morocco. Having plundered his country for more than thirty years, he will die three months later of advanced and untreated prostate cancer.

17
MAY

1809
Napoleon orders the annexation of all papal states to the French Empire.

1900
After a 217-day siege by the Boer Army in the Second Boer War, British forces under Robert Baden-Powell are relieved at Mafeking.

1902
Greek archaeologist Valerios Stais discovers the Antikythera Mechanism, which is revealed to be a highly accurate analogue computer designed to predict astronomical eclipses dating to the first century BC.

1916
The Daylight Savings Act, by which the clocks move forward by one hour in summer and back again in autumn, is adopted in British law on the advice of William Willett. The resulting savings on lighting costs were particularly attractive during the coal shortages of the First World War.

1983
Israel signs agreements for it to withdraw all its forces from southern Lebanon.

2007
For the first time since 1953, train traffic is allowed to flow both ways across the 38th Parallel dividing North and South Korea.

18
MAY

1974
The 2,120 feet (646 m) Warsaw Radio Mast is completed and is the tallest structure in the world until its spectacular collapse in 1991. Promptly rebuilt, it will remain the tallest structure until completion of the Burj Khalifa in Dubai in 2010.

1987
At the height of the Iran-Iraq War, USS *Stark* is monitoring the conflict from the waters of the Arabian Gulf when it is hit by two Iraqi missiles, causing the deaths of thirty-seven United States Navy personnel and injuring twenty-one others. Baghdad apologizes for the mistake.

1990
East and West Germany take a step closer to unification as the two respective countries agree to use the West German Mark as of 1 July.

2005
Transmissions from the Hubble Space Telescope today and on 15 May confirm the existence of Nix and Hydra, two extra moons for Pluto.

2009
The Sri Lankan Government announces the defeat of the Tamil Tigers who, for the past twenty-six years, have been waging a campaign for a self-governing Tamil sector in the north of the island.

19
MAY

1536

Accused of adultery with several men including her own brother, Anne Boleyn, the second wife of King Henry VIII of England, is beheaded. The following day Henry VIII will become betrothed to her lady-in-waiting, Jane Seymour.

1898

William Gladstone, the Grand Old Man of British politics, dies.

1910

French astronomer Nicolas Camille Flammarion has pronounced that when Halley's Comet returns today the tail-gasses will exterminate all life on earth. Thousands buy protection in the form of 'comet pills' and 'comet umbrellas' while others congregate in churches to await the end of the world.

1935

British Army officer T.E. Lawrence (of Arabia) crashes his motorbike in Dorset and dies. His liaison role in the Arab Revolt against the Ottoman Turks between 1916 and 1918, as described in his autobiographical account *Seven Pillars of Wisdom*, earned him the status of a hero and champion of the Arab cause, but he has had harsh critics too: Oxford historian Hugh Trevor Roper dismissed him as a fraud, a charlatan and a fantasist.

1982

Multi-award-winning Italian actress Sophia Loren is sent to prison for a month in Naples for tax offences.

20
MAY

1506

Having fallen from favour, Genoese explorer and navigator Christopher Columbus dies penniless in Spain, apparently still sure on his deathbed that his voyages had taken him to the East Indies (South and South East Asia) even though he was in the Americas.

1802

Executing something of a humanitarian U-turn, France under Napoleon Bonaparte restores legality to slavery throughout France's colonial possessions.

1873

A Latvian-Jewish immigrant tailor, Jacob Davis, and a German-Jewish immigrant businessman, Levi Strauss, take out a patent on Davis's design of jeans with copper-riveted pockets. It is Davis who came up with the idea for tough trousers for miners in the gold fields; Strauss was only the fabric supplier but he will eventually take over the entire venture.

1980

To the ire of hard-line French Canadians, the Quebec Referendum today rejects the motion to quit the Federation of Canada and become independent.

2002

East Timor celebrates independence from Indonesia.

21

MAY

1502

Sailing under the Portuguese flag, explorer João da Nova discovers the remote island of St Helena, where Napoleon will one day reside.

1804

Destined to become the last resting place of Molière, Oscar Wilde and American singer-songwriter Jim Morrison, Père Lachaise cemetery in Paris opens its gates today.

1927

American pilot Charles Lindbergh flying from New York touches down at Le Bourget Airport, outside Paris, to claim the $25,000 prize offered to the first person to undertake a solo transatlantic flight.

1945

Humphrey Bogart, forty-five, marries the nineteen-year-old Lauren Bacall. They had met the previous year on the set of *To Have and Have Not*.

1991

Former Prime Minister of India, Rajiv Gandhi, is assassinated in Tamil Nadu, India. A young woman, later identified as Thenmozhi Rajaratnam of the Tamil Tigers, bent to kiss his feet and then detonated her suicide pack.

22
MAY

1906

The Wright Brothers, aviation pioneers in America, are granted Patent 821,393 for their Flying Machine.

1945

Operation Paperclip is given the go-ahead to whitewash Nazi scientists and resettle them in America, often with new identities. Many end up in NASA but doctors involved in experiments using concentration camp human test subjects are also brought out for the knowledge they have gained, as indeed are bio-warfare experts and Gestapo interrogators.

1960

The most powerful earthquake ever recorded at Magnitude 9.5 hits Chile, triggering tsunamis that inflict death and destruction in Japan, Hawaii, the Philippines, Hong Kong and New Zealand.

1963

The Greek anti-fascist politician Grigoris Lambrakis is clubbed to the ground by fascists, dying three days later of brain injuries. The Athens Classic Marathon will be run in his honour forever after.

2002

Finally brought to justice, Ku Klux Klansman Bobby Frank Cherry is convicted in Birmingham, Alabama, USA, for the 1963 bombing of the 16th Street Baptist Church in which four young African-American women were killed. Laughing and joking throughout the trial, he will die in prison.

23
MAY

1701

Leaving optimists forever searching for his supposed buried treasure, the Scottish pirate Captain Kidd is today hanged in London. The first noose snaps but the second holds firm and his body is left on grisly display in a cage hung over the Thames.

1794

Maximilien de Robespierre, the French Revolutionary leader, survives an assassination attempt by royalist Cécile Renault.

1887

Revolutionary France puts the crown jewels up for sale today to raise a badly needed six million francs.

1934

Aged twenty-three and twenty-five respectively, American outlaws Bonnie Elizabeth Parker and Clyde Chestnut Barrow die in a police ambush in Louisiana. Bonnie's husband, Roy Thornton, was in prison when she met Clyde but she never divorced him even though she was smitten with Clyde.

1977

Nine Moluccan terrorists from the Maluku Islands take over a Dutch train at Assen as four others take over a nearby primary school. Demanding independence for their islands, which will soon merge with Indonesia, the siege lasts twenty days until troops storm the train and the school; two hostages and six Moluccans are killed.

24
MAY

1809

Dartmoor Prison is completed and opens up as a detention point for French prisoners from the Napoleonic Wars. The guests bring with them the game of dominoes, which is spreading across Europe.

1830

The nursery rhyme 'Mary had a Little Lamb' by Sarah Josepha Hale is published by American publishers in Boston. The poem celebrates her childhood friend, Mary Sawyer of Sterling, Massachusetts, who really did have a pet lamb that followed her to school. It became the first-ever recorded verse when Thomas Edison famously recorded it in 1877 using his invention of the phonograph.

1975

The first batch of eighty Western journalists and cameramen is allowed to evacuate the fallen city of Saigon (now Ho Chi Minh City), leaving 16,000 other foreign nationals to ponder their fate under the North Vietnamese occupying forces.

2001

In the Israeli town of Talpiot, Jerusalem, nearly 700 guests are packed into the Versailles Wedding Hall when the main floor gives way. At least 23 are killed outright and more than 300 are injured, making it Israel's worst civil disaster.

25
MAY

1787

With George Washington presiding, the Constitutional Convention begins in Philadelphia to agree how to govern the USA following independence from Britain. Slavery, still widespread at the time, will prove a controversial issue especially in the southern States; the compromise agreed will be to give Congress the power to ban the international slave trade, but not for another twenty years.

1810

Today sees the start of the May Revolution in Argentina as people and the military unite to kick out the Spanish Viceroy, signifying the beginning of their War of Independence.

1837

French Canadians of Quebec Province rise up in armed revolt at British control but are soon suppressed.

1935

At the Big Ten Championships in Ann Arbor, Michigan, USA, African-American athlete Jesse Owens breaks three world records – long jump, 220-yard sprint and 220-yard hurdles. He will go on to win four gold medals at the 1936 Olympics.

1961

American President John F. Kennedy makes his famous address to Congress, promising to put a man on the moon before the end of the decade.

26
MAY

1637

The true birth of Thanksgiving. A conflict between the Pequot tribe and an alliance of other Native American tribes and colonists leads to a mass slaughter of 700 Pequot women, children and elders by the English colonists of Massachusetts while the Pequot warriors are away from their camp. Governor John Winthrop will declare this the first official Thanksgiving Day to celebrate the subduing of the Pequots. This annual 'celebration' day will be shifted to November under President Lincoln.

1805

Napoleon accepts the Italian Crown in Milan to become Emperor of the French and King of Italy.

1865

With the American Civil War officially ended by declaration on 10 May, one of the last of the Confederate forces surrenders under General Edmund Kirby Smith.

1908

A speculative drilling team at Masjed Soleyman in Persia (now Iran) make the first oil strike in the Middle East to initiate a dramatic shift in the global balance of power.

1940

The first ships sail out from Britain to evacuate the troops trapped at Dunkirk in France during the Second World War.

27
MAY

1679

The concept of *habeas corpus*, meaning no individual may be detained without trial, is enshrined in English law by King Charles II.

1703

Tsar Peter the Great founds a new city in Russia proclaiming that, when finished, it will be called St Petersburg and be the nation's capital. It will retain that status until 1918 when the Revolutionaries transfer the government to Moscow.

1900

Belgium becomes the first country to elect a government based on the system of proportional representation by the different political parties.

1937

San Francisco's Golden Gate Bridge is opened today amid much ceremony and 200,000 people crossing by foot and on roller skates.

1965

American animator and business magnate Walt Disney acquires vast tracts of land outside Orlando in Florida in readiness for his Disney World project. All the land deals are signed using anonymous land trusts to mask the identity of the buyer and prevent a hike in prices.

28
MAY

1588

The Spanish Armada sets out from Lisbon for England. Contrary to popular perception, the defenders had many more ships than the Spanish and there was little engagement in battle. Harried by the English fleet up the east coast of England, many of the Spanish ships will be run aground or lost during storms.

1932

In order to protect land from flooding, the Dutch complete the world's longest dam of 20 miles (32 km); this creates a fresh-water lake (the IJsselmeer) out of what was the Zuiderzee, a natural salt-water inlet.

1934

The first to survive infancy, the Dionne Quintuplets are born today in Callander, Ontario, Canada. Their shocked mother, Elzire, thought she was carrying twins. From birth the girls will be a massive tourist attraction; the Ontario government will take their custody, housing them in a purpose-built nursery with an observation gallery for tourists. Later the government will pay compensation to the sisters for exploiting them.

1942

Reprisals across Czechoslovakia begin in the wake of the assassination of Nazi official Reinhard Heydrich in Prague the previous day. Intelligence will falsely link the assassins to the villages of Lidice and Ležáky, and soon every living soul there will be murdered or transported and the villages razed to the ground.

29
MAY

1453

Following a siege lasting more than a year, the Byzantine Empire collapses with the fall of Constantinople to the Turkish Army.

1871

Today is a Monday and the first bank holiday celebrated in Britain.

1953

New Zealand mountaineer Edmund Hillary and Nepalese Sherpa Tenzing Norgay conquer Everest.

1979

Bishop Abel Muzorewa becomes the first black prime minister of Rhodesia which will, within weeks, rename itself Zimbabwe-Rhodesia.

1982

Pope John Paul II makes the first papal visit to Britain. It is 450 years since King Henry VIII seized all monastic properties in the realm and set up the Church of England.

1985

Just before the European Cup Final kicks off, English (Liverpool) supporters mount a full-scale charge on Italian (Juventus) fans in the Heysel Stadium in Belgium, killing 39 and putting another 620 in hospital. Mounted police are required to break up the incident after which fourteen will stand trial for manslaughter with English teams banned from European competitions for five years.

30
MAY

1431

French heroine Joan of Arc is burned at the stake in the marketplace of Rouen, condemned on a charge of heresy by a pro-English tribunal.

1593

Stabbed above his right eye, Christopher Marlowe is murdered in a pub in London. A contemporary poet and playwright of Shakespeare, Marlowe allegedly also worked for Queen Elizabeth I's spymaster, Sir Francis Walsingham, but whether the stabbing was connected to this role has never been established.

1911

The new high-speed motor endurance race, the Indianapolis 500-Mile, held in Indiana, USA, is won today by Ray Harroun in his Marmon Wasp, the first car ever to be fitted with his own invention of a rear-view mirror.

1959

The first hovercraft, as designed and built by English engineer Sir Christopher Cockerell, is tested on the beach and waters at Cowes on the Isle of Wight.

1972

Sub-contract terrorism is born when three members of the Japanese Red Army walk through Lod Airport in Tel Aviv, Israel, spraying gunfire to kill twenty-six. The group has close ties to the Popular Front for the Liberation of Palestine (PFLP).

31
MAY

1669

Failing eyesight forces Samuel Pepys to pen the last entry in his diary today, the last words asking God to prepare him for his death.

1891

Construction begins on the Trans-Siberian Railway.

1895

American doctor John Harvey Kellogg files an application for a patent for his Corn Flakes breakfast food. Believing diet to be the key to a healthy mind, Kellogg launches his flakes as part of his crusade to stop the young of America indulging in solitary sexual activity.

1902

The Second Boer War ends with British victory. British Army Officer Kitchener puts the inhabitants of all Boer-supporting towns and villages into concentration camps – the first use of the term. More than 30,000 Boer civilians will die in the camps and an unknown number of black Africans.

2004

Alberta Martin, one of the oldest recipients of the Civil War Widow's pension, dies today aged ninety-seven in Alabama, USA. In a not-uncommon practice, she was twenty-one in 1927 when she married the eighty-one-year-old Confederate Pensioner William Martin Jarvis to gain rights to his $50 pension as financial security for her son by a previous marriage.

1
JUNE

1660
Mary Dyer becomes the first woman executed for religion in America when she is hanged by the Puritans for being a Quaker.

1815
Napoleon Bonaparte swears his allegiance to the Constitution of France.

1879
Napoleon Eugene dies in a British uniform fighting the Zulus, so ending the French imperial line.

1943
KLM Flight 777 out of neutral Lisbon is shot down in the Bay of Biscay by a swarm of German fighters. Berlin knew Churchill was making his way back from North Africa and on that flight is English actor Leslie Howard and his portly, cigar-puffing agent, Alfred Chenhalls, who together looked remarkably like Churchill and his bodyguard Walter H. Thompson.

2001
Having been told he will have to abdicate claim to the throne if he marries the Indian woman he loves, Nepali Crown Prince Dipendra slaughters nine members of the royal family, including his own parents, at their weekly family dinner. Shooting himself afterwards, and dying three days later, he leaves Nepal in a rudderless state of chaos.

2

JUNE

455

The Vandals enter Rome and spend the next two weeks stealing anything of value and destroying countless buildings, thereby leaving their tribal name to posterity as a synonym for such behaviour.

1882

Italian General Giuseppe Garibaldi dies peacefully today. His volunteer force's famous red shirts came about by accident when the Uruguay Government gave him a consignment of such garments seized from a bankrupt who was to ship them out to slaughterhouse workers in Argentina. Everybody copied Garibaldi, making red the favourite colour of left-wing activists ever since.

1946

In a constitutional referendum, Italy abolishes the monarchy and declares the country a Republic.

1953

The coronation of Queen Elizabeth II in Westminster, London. The announcement that the ceremony would be televised helped to sell more than 1 million television licences during the year of the event.

1964

The Palestine Liberation Organization (PLO) is formed in Jerusalem with the aim of creating an independent State of Palestine.

3

JUNE

1898

The Seaman's Saviour, Samuel Plimsoll, dies in Folkestone, England. At his instigation all ships have a white Plimsoll Line painted on the hull to mark the depth to which they can be loaded with cargo to prevent catastrophic overloading. When white tennis shoes make an appearance they will pick up the nickname as, like the Plimsoll Line, if water gets above the white band joining the upper to the sole of the shoe, then the wearer gets wet.

1940

Nazi diplomat Franz Rademacher unveils his Madagascar Plan, where all surviving European Jews will be forcibly deported to that island after the War to establish an isolated Jewish homeland.

1942

The Japanese begin their invasion of Alaska with the capture of the strategically important offshore islands of Attu and Kiska. Some 6,000 Japanese troops will remain here, dug-in on American soil, for nearly a year, prompting the rapid completion of the Alaskan Highway as an American supply route during the War, eventually to open to civilian traffic in 1948.

1968

Feminist radical, Valerie Solanas, gets her fifteen minutes of fame when she shoots Andy Warhol through the chest. It left Warhol, who barely survived, having to wear a surgical corset for the rest of his life.

4
JUNE

1798

Supposedly the world's greatest lover, Italian adventurer Giacomo Casanova dies in exile in Bohemia. His memoirs describe his numerous affairs; in fact, he was no more promiscuous than many upper-class Europeans at that time.

1855

Major Henry Wayne sails for North Africa to buy the stock to set up the United States Camel Corps, intended for military use in the USA. Upon his return, the Corps decides to prove its worth by opening up a new route across the country from St Louis, through Flagstaff, Arizona, and down to San Bernardino in California – just as the song says, for this was the birth of Route 66.

1913

English suffragette Emily Davison is killed as she runs onto the course at Epsom to grab the bridle of King George V's horse as it runs the Derby. The horse, Anmer, is brought down, injuring jockey Herbert Jones to whom Queen Mary writes to say she hopes he is not too badly injured by the 'abominable conduct of a brutal lunatic woman'.

1989

Sparks from the wheels of two trains passing each other on the Trans-Siberian Railway ignite gas from a trackside pipeline leak with nearly 600 dying in the resulting fireball. Many of the casualties are children as both trains were serving the Black Sea holiday resort.

5

JUNE

1661
Leading light in Europe's Scientific Revolution, physicist Isaac Newton is admitted to Trinity College, Cambridge, despite his mother's objections; she wants him to stay at home and farm.

1941
The Japanese carry out the relatively unknown terror-bombing of the Chinese city of Chongqing and the 4,000 who seek refuge in a railway tunnel all die of suffocation. America, still neutral in the War at the time, ceases the sale of aviation parts and supplies to Japan. In 2006, a group of forty survivors of the bombing demand compensation and apologies from Tokyo.

1956
Elvis Presley goes on television to promote his new single 'Hound Dog' on *The Milton Berle Show*, scandalizing Middle America with his 'suggestive hip movements'.

1972
Having died in Paris on 28 May, The Duke of Windsor, one-time King Edward VIII, is buried quietly at Frogmore, Windsor. It will be another fourteen years before his wife, Wallis Simpson, joins him there.

6
JUNE

1844

English draper George Williams founds the Young Men's Christian Association (YMCA). The Industrial Revolution is attracting numerous young men from the countryside and Williams is determined to keep them out of the taverns and brothels so he founds his organization for apprentices of the drapery and embroidery guilds and other houses of business.

1944

D-Day and the first landing craft hit the Normandy beaches in the Allied invasion of Normandy, France, during the Second World War. At the same time, Leonard Dawe, schoolmaster and crossword compiler for the *Daily Telegraph*, is grilled by MI5. In the preceding weeks his grids have included the answers of Juno, Gold, Sword, Omaha and Utah – codenames for the landing beaches – and other operational code words such as Overlord, Mulberry and Neptune. Initially fearing Dawe to be an enemy operative, the case will finally be cracked in 1984 when a schoolboy taught by Dawe owns up to having supplied the words to his teacher having heard them from Canadian and American soldiers camped nearby.

1984

India's Prime Minister Indira Gandhi orders troops to storm the Golden Temple of Amritsar in the Punjab, which has been under the control of Sikh militants for the past few days. In the ensuing battle nearly 500 militants and civilians and 83 of the attacking troops will be killed.

7
JUNE

1329

Death of King of the Scots Robert the Bruce, who fought successfully to regain Scotland's independence from England. Allegedly he died from leprosy, a common disease in Britain at the time.

1899

Temperance activist Carrie Nation marches into Dobson's Saloon in Kiowa, Kansas, and reduces it to rubble with her axe. Her actions will put 'battle-axe' into the English language.

1929

Mussolini and Pope Pius XI sign the Lateran Treaty, which brings the Vatican State into existence.

1973

At the invitation of Israeli Prime Minister Mrs Golda Meir, German Chancellor Willy Brandt today makes an emotional visit to Israel to lay a wreath at the Yad Vashem Holocaust Memorial.

1998

In Jasper, Texas, neo-Nazi white supremacists Shawn Berry, Lawrence Brewer and John King kill the African-American James Byrd by tying him to the back of their pick-up and dragging him through the streets for three miles. Before his execution by lethal injection, Brewer will order a ridiculously large meal that he does not touch, prompting Texas to abandon the tradition of the condemned man's Last Meal.

8

632

Mohammed ('Peace Be Upon Him'), prophet and founder of Islam, dies in Medina (in present-day Saudi Arabia).

793

The first Viking raid on the British Isles takes place when the monastery on Lindisfarne, off the north-east coast, is attacked with considerable brutality. The raiders are of the warrior-elite Berserkers, or bear-shirts, famed for their savagery that puts 'going berserk' into the English language.

1874

After many campaigns, the Apache chief Cochise (meaning 'hard as oak') dies in New Mexico.

1949

The George Orwell classic *Nineteen Eighty-Four* is published. The English author is said to have chosen the title as a permutation of 1948, the year in which it was written.

1985

Brazilian police announce that they have the body of Auschwitz's 'Angel of Death', Josef Mengele. He had drowned as the result of a stroke while swimming in the coastal resort of Bertioga in 1979 and had been been buried under the name of Wolfgang Gerhard in Embu das Artes.

9
JUNE

68
Bereft of support in all quarters, Roman Emperor Nero stabs himself to death.

1534
The French explorer Jacques Cartier is the first European to discover the St Lawrence River in present-day Quebec, Canada.

1865
The passionate affair between celebrated English author Charles Dickens and Ellen Ternan, an actress half his age, attracts attention when the train in which they are returning from a discreet holiday in France is derailed at Staplehurst Viaduct in Kent, killing ten and injuring forty. Leaving *The Mystery of Edwin Drood* unfinished, Dickens will die five years later, almost to the hour.

1934
Donald Duck makes his debut today in *The Wise Little Hen*. Many critics will soon point out that it really should be Donald Drake.

2010
The Nadahan wedding-bomb atrocity occurrs in Kandahar, Afghanistan. In keeping with tradition, the men and women are celebrating the marriage in separate areas when a suicide bomber wanders in to the men-only celebrations and triggers his device to kill at least forty of those present and maim another eighty. Most shocking of all is that the atrocity is committed by a twelve-year-old boy.

10
JUNE

1793
The world's first public zoo opens today at the Jardin des Plantes in Paris.

1829
Rivalry between English Universities of Oxford and Cambridge goes water-born after the first Boat Race is organized by Charles Wordsworth, nephew of the famous poet.

1965
A British European Airways aeroplane on the Paris-London run makes the world's first fully automatic landing at London Heathrow.

1967
The Six-Day War between Israel and its neighbours ends, leaving Israel in control of three times as much territory than it held at the outbreak.

1991
About 20,000 American service personnel have to evacuate Clarke Air Base on the Philippines after the long-dormant Mount Pinatubo wakes up, showering the area with ash and other volcanic debris.

2000
London's Millennium Bridge is opened but closes soon after pending engineers' reports on why it sways so violently when loaded with pedestrian traffic.

11
JUNE

1509

King of England Henry VIII marries his widowed sister-in-law, Catherine of Aragon, behind closed doors at Greenwich in defiance of clerics who point to Leviticus 20:21 which denounces such unions as impure and doomed.

1955

There is terror on the track at Le Mans when a Mercedes competing in the twenty-four-hour Grand Prix sideswipes another car on the Tribune Straights causing it to go airborne and fly into the grandstand. The magnesium in the panels of the car's body explodes in a fireball that kills the driver and 83 spectators, with 120 more suffering horrific burns and injuries.

1964

Shortly after 9 am this morning, Walter Seifert enters the Volkhoven Catholic Primary School near Cologne, Germany, with a homemade flame-thrower that he uses to kill two teachers and eight children, injuring twenty-two others. After poisoning himself in a suicide bid at the scene, he is shot by police and dies later in hospital.

1979

American actor Marion Morrison, better known as John Wayne, dies today. His nickname 'The Duke' derived in his childhood when he delivered newspapers with his Airedale dog called Duke, the inseparable pair being known locally as Big Duke and Little Duke.

12

JUNE

1902

Horn & Hardart open their first waiter-less food service automat in Philadelphia, becoming America's first fast-food chain. They had taken inspiration from a trip to Berlin to study the Quisisana, the first-ever such 'restaurant' in which the customers file obediently past a bank of glass-fronted cabinets, removing whatever dish takes their fancy.

1931

American Prohibition agent Eliot Ness and his team of law enforcement officers, nicknamed the Untouchables, help nail gangster Al Capone for tax infringements.

1942

German Jewish girl Anne Frank is given a diary for her thirteenth birthday and history will forever be changed.

1979

Bryan Allen scoops the £100,000 prize offered for the first man-powered flight across the English Channel. Pedalling frantically for nearly three hours, he powers the Gossamer Albatross across the water at a height of about 5 feet (1.5 m).

1991

The residents of Leningrad vote overwhelmingly in favour of reverting back to the pre-Revolutionary name of St Petersburg.

13
JUNE

323BC

Alexander the Great dies, leaving his generals to fight over portions of his empire. Ptolemy I Soter grabs Egypt to establish the dynasty that will produce Cleopatra, who was herself Greek and not Egyptian.

1381

Wat Tyler leads the Peasants' Revolt of agricultural workers and craftsmen on a march to London to oppose the institution of a poll tax.

1892

Basil Rathbone, the English actor who gave Sherlock Holmes his trademark deerstalker, is born today in South Africa. During the First World War he will disguise himself as a tree to get near to German lines and pick up information.

1900

Dedicated to ridding China of all foreign influence and interference, the first contingent of the Boxer Rebellion march into Beijing today and make their way to the foreign quarter where they murder Sugiyama Akira of the Japanese legation.

1944

The first of 9,521 V-1 bombs is launched from Occupied France to hit Mile End in London. The nickname of Doodlebug will come from Americans in London who use the term back home for mini-racing cars with open exhausts that make a noise similar to the rasping note of the V-1's ramjet.

14
JUNE

1800

Napoleon is victorious over the Austrians at the Battle of Marengo. After the battle he allegedly sits down to a new dish of chicken and crayfish, which has forever more been aptly titled Chicken Marengo.

1900

Hawaii becomes a United States Territory.

1940

The Germans have taken Paris and today the Nazi flag flies from the top of the Eiffel Tower. With Charles de Gaulle in exile in Britain, the collaborative Vichy Government is set up under French General, Marshal Pétain, whose outstanding military record from the First World War, particularly during the Battle of Verdun, has earned him hero status. However, after the Second World War he will be tried for treason and, on conviction, stripped of all military honours and jailed.

1964

Anti-Apartheid leader Nelson Mandela is sentenced to life imprisonment on Robben Island, a few miles off the Cape Town coast.

1967

China tests its first hydrogen bomb.

1982

Argentinean forces formally surrender to the British in the Falklands.

15
JUNE

1215

The Council of Barons force King John to agree the Magna Carta, the charter considered to be the first step towards a constitution for England. Doing little for the common man, the document puts more power into the hands of the barons, who have become disenchanted with the king after unsuccessful wars and higher taxes.

1860

Florence Nightingale opens the world's first school for nurses in St Thomas' Hospital, London. In popular culture she has become a hero, celebrated as 'The Lady with the Lamp' for her nighttime rounds of the wards when she served in the Crimea.

1919

John Alcock and Arthur Brown land at Clifden in Ireland having completed the first non-stop transatlantic flight.

1934

Hitler and Mussolini meet for the first time in Venice. Neither seemed impressed – Hitler thought Mussolini was a pompous buffoon and Mussolini described Hitler as a mad little clown.

1954

American physicist and atomic weapons consultant Robert Oppenheimer is declared a security risk by the Committee of Un-American Activities and will have his top-secret security clearance revoked. Also suspected of being a Moscow mole, he will be spied on and monitored for the rest of his life.

16
JUNE

1958

Soviet Chairman Nikita Khrushchev orders the execution of former Chairman Imre Nagy of Hungary for his leadership of the anti-Soviet uprising crushed by Soviet troops two years ago. According to a Kremlin insider, he was executed 'as a lesson to all other leaders in socialist countries'.

1963

Russian cosmonaut Valentina Tereshkova becomes the first woman in space as she lifts off in the Soviet Vostok 6. Spending three days in space and orbiting the earth forty-eight times, Tereshkova racks up more space-hours than all American astronauts put together before this date.

1972

West German police capture Ulrike Meinhof, the last member still at large of the left-wing terrorist Red Army Faction known as the Baader-Meinhof Group. Before her trial concludes she will be found hanged in her prison cell in 1976.

1977

German 'Father of Rocket Science' Wernher von Braun dies today. To endear him to the American public, the CIA and NASA had to airbrush out the fact that he had in fact been a Nazi SS Major during the Second World War, who used slave labour in his rocket factories where more died making his V-2s than the rockets themselves killed.

17
JUNE

1775

The first major battle of the American War of Independence is scheduled to take place at Bunker Hill, north of Boston, but the American forces dig-in on nearby Breed's Hill instead. So, it will be atop Breed's Hill that the granite Bunker Hill Memorial will be erected in 1843 by Sarah Josepha Hale, the author of 'Mary Had a Little Lamb'.

1867

In the Glasgow Royal Infirmary, British surgeon Joseph Lister performs a mastectomy on his sister using carbolic acid, becoming the first to use antiseptics in surgery.

1939

The last public beheading in France happens today when murderer Eugen Weidmann is executed on a guillotine set up outside the Saint-Pierre prison in Versailles. Such is the hysterical behaviour of the crowd that French President Albert Lebrun decrees there is to be no more such public 'entertainment'. Also in the crowd is the seventeen-year-old English actor-to-be Christopher Lee, on whom the incident will have a lasting effect.

1972

Five men are arrested after breaking into the Watergate Complex, currently being used by the Democrat Party in the run-up to the next presidential election. Caught with all sorts of surveillance gear and bugs, all will be identified as working for Nixon's ill-advisedly named CREEP, or Campaign to Re-Elect the President.

18
JUNE

1815

The English Duke of Wellington, supported by a Prussian army, defeats French Emperor Napoleon Bonaparte at the Battle of Waterloo. Financier Nathan Rothschild has in place a network of fast-riding couriers and hears of the victory a full day before the British Government, time he puts to profitable use dealing on the London Stock Exchange and making massive gains.

1873

American suffragette Susan B. Anthony is fined $100 in court for having tried to vote in the 1872 presidential election between incumbent President Ulysses S. Grant and Democrat Horace Greeley. She counters with a petition against the government for the infringement of her rights under the Fourteenth Amendment.

1979

Soviet leader Leonid Brezhnev meets with US President Jimmy Carter in the Imperial Hofburg Palace in Vienna to sign the Strategic Arms Limitations Talks Treaty. The signing done, Carter flings his arms round the stony-faced Russian and kisses him on both cheeks to show his delight, much to Brezhnev's chagrin.

1983

The seventeen-year-old Mona Mahmudnizhad and nine other women are hanged today on a polo field in Shiraz, Iran, for their refusal to abandon their Bahá'í faith. All have to be carried to their death as they are incapable of walking after being repeatedly whipped on the soles of their feet.

19
JUNE

1790

The French National Assembly abolishes all hereditary titles.

1829

Sir Robert Peel establishes the London Metropolitan Police in Whitehall Place. The building is accessed by a yard called Scotland Yard, which has now become synonymous with the institution.

1846

The Elysian Fields in Hoboken, New Jersey, USA, host the first ever official baseball match, complete with the new regulation layout, between the New York Nine and the Knickerbocker Club, with the former winning.

1867

Despite the likes of French writer Victor Hugo and Italian General Garibaldi sending telegrams begging for clemency, the Revolutionary Mexican Government nevertheless put deposed Emperor Maximilian up against a wall and shoot him.

1910

Father's Day is instituted in the city of Spokane in Washington State, USA, by Sonora Dodd, determined to honour her father for raising her and her five siblings almost singlehandedly.

20
JUNE

1819

Proving the critics wrong, the American hybrid sailing/steamer SS *Savannah* becomes the first steamship to cross the Atlantic, taking twenty-nine days to make it from Georgia to Liverpool. It had long been argued that no ship could carry enough fuel to complete the trip.

1837

The teenage Victoria ascends the British throne on the death of her uncle, William IV.

1893

On the day after her thirty-third birthday, Lizzie Borden is acquitted of the axe-murder of her father and stepmother. A cause célèbre at the time, the couple were hacked to death at the family home in Fall River, Massachusetts, USA, and the crime will never be solved.

1949

American tennis star, Gussie Moran, is the first to challenge the Wimbledon dress code at the All England Club in London when she marches onto court today in a short tennis skirt that does little to obscure her frilly knickers, designed to be seen. Though it gets a good reception from the fans and the press, the Wimbledon Committee begrudge that 'sin and vulgarity' are invading the game.

21
JUNE

1675

With the previous edifice destroyed in the Great Fire of London in 1666, work begins today on the new St Paul's Cathedral under the guidance and design of Sir Christopher Wren.

1791

Reacting to the revolutionary mood in France, the French royal family escape but are captured in Varennes and brought back to Paris under guard.

1876

Mexican General Antonio López de Santa Anna, best known for his attack on the Alamo in the Texas Revolution, dies today in abject poverty. In exile after the war and in partnership with Thomas Adams, he had organized the first shipments to New York of *chicle*, a natural gum intended as a substitute for rubber. Adams used it instead to develop chewing gum.

1919

Having surrendered themselves to the British Navy in Scapa Flow in the Orkneys, Scotland, the Commanders of the German fleet open the seacocks to wreck their battleships and cruisers in order to prevent their later use against Germany.

2009

Although technically remaining within the Kingdom of Denmark, Greenland issues notice that as of today it is assuming self-determination.

22
JUNE

1611

Tired of the hardships of helping English navigator Henry Hudson find his elusive Northwest Passage to China through the frozen wastes, the crew of *Discovery* decide to mutiny and set the indignant Hudson, his son and seven others adrift in a small boat, never to be seen again.

1987

Born Fred Austerlitz, Fred Astaire dies today aged a nimble eighty-eight. After his first audition at RKO Radio Pictures, the notes reportedly read, 'Can't sing. Can't act. Can dance a little.'

1990

Featured in countless spy movies and a feature of the Cold War, Berlin's Checkpoint Charlie is today dismantled after the fall of the Berlin Wall the year before.

2004

Belgian child-rapist and killer, Marc Dutroux, is handed down a life sentence with no hope of parole. He had detained a number of girls in his converted basement, raping and murdering them before burying the remains on the property.

23
JUNE

1914

Pancho Villa captures the city of Zacatecas in the Mexican Revolutionary War, becoming the only military leader to fight under a film contract. In January 1914 he had signed an agreement giving the Mutual Film Company of California exclusive rights to film his troops in battle in exchange for $25,000 and a share of the profits.

1942

German pilot Armin Faber lands by mistake at RAF Pembrey in Wales, thinking he is in Northern France after mistaking the Bristol Channel for the English Channel. In 1944, Faber manages to fool his captors into repatriating him by feigning epilepsy and is soon back flying front-line missions.

1959

While attention was wrongly focused on American physicist Robert Oppenheimer as the security risk on the Manhattan Bomb Project to produce atomic bombs, the real spy, German physicist Klaus Fuchs, was hard at work. He is released today after serving nine years of his fourteen-year prison sentence and is allowed to leave for Dresden in East Germany.

1980

Sanjay Gandhi, son of the prime minister of India, Indira, is killed in a plane crash. Impressing spectators at the Delhi Flying Club, he attempts to loop-the-loop over the clubhouse but loses control and flies into the ground.

24
JUNE

1519

Vilified by history, Lucrezia Borgia, daughter of Pope Alexander VI, dies today. Invariably portrayed in film and fiction as a femme fatale, much given to murder and intrigue, very little is actually known about her and her involvement in the machinations of her Renaissance Italian family. Among her descendants is King Juan Carlos of Spain.

1859

French and Austrian armies clash at the Battle of Solferino in Italy and the horrendous aftermath of the dead and mutilated, abandoned where they have fallen, is witnessed by the Swiss businessman Jean-Henri Dunant who is touring Lombardy at the time. Disgusted by what he sees, Dunant returns home and sets up the International Committee of the Red Cross, now The Red Cross, and is credited for inspiring the creation of the Geneva Convention.

1947

American aviator Kenneth Arnold, flying past Mount Rainier in Washington State, reports being paced by a flight of nine UFOs that he describes as pie-dish or saucer-shaped. The press opts for the term 'flying saucer', now very much part of UFO vernacular.

1990

Kathleen Young and Irene Templeton become the first women ordained into the Anglican Church in a ceremony at St Anne's Cathedral, Belfast, Northern Ireland.

25
JUNE

1876

Expecting little opposition, Lieutenant Colonel George Custer rides to the encampment at the Little Bighorn River, Montana, USA, during the American Indian Wars, unaware that there are more than 2,000 Native American armed warriors ready to counter-attack. The US troopers in three battalions are rapidly cut down, with Custer's men making a final stand by shooting their horses to provide a temporary defence barrier, before they succumb to the onslaught, hence the battle's popular name, 'Custer's Last Stand'.

1903

Marie Curie presents her thesis to the University of Paris, announcing her discovery of the radium that will eventually kill her. She habitually carried samples around in her pocket and noted with amusement how they glowed in the dark. All of her papers and possessions are still so radioactive that viewers have to suit-up to view them to this day.

1950

North Korean leader Kim Il-Sung sends his troops over the 38th Parallel and into South Korea to start the three-year war involving China and the Soviet Union (supporting North Korea) and the United Nations led by America (supporting South Korea).

2009

Michael Jackson goes into cardiac arrest and dies in Los Angeles after 'over-medication' administered by his personal physician.

26
JUNE

1857

In Hyde Park in London, Queen Victoria awards the first sixty-two Victoria Crosses, the highest award for wartime valour for British and Commonwealth forces.

1870

The United States finally makes Christmas Day a public holiday. Scotland, where New Year celebrations have long been deemed the more important, will not make Christmas Day a public holiday until 1957, and England, where the accent is more on Christmas, will not make New Year's Day a bank holiday until 1974.

1906

The public roads around the French city of Le Mans are closed for the first French Grand Prix. It is won by the Hungarian entrant, Ferenc Szisz, with a recorded average speed of 63 mph (101 kph).

1974

The barcode is used for the first time to scan a pack of Wrigley's chewing gum at the checkout of the Marsh Supermarket in Troy, Ohio, USA.

1993

In retaliation for a failed assassination attempt on the life of former American President George W. Bush in Kuwait back in April, the US mount a series of Tomahawk missile strikes on Iraqi Intelligence offices in and around Baghdad.

27
JUNE

1778

Having been hidden under the floor of the Zion Reformed Church in Allentown, Pennsylvania, throughout the American War of Independence, the Liberty Bell is returned to its rightful place in Philadelphia.

1939

Pan-American Airways begins operation of the first scheduled transatlantic flying-boat service that terminates at Foynes in Ireland. The planes are neither heated nor pressurized so Pan-Am ground staff greet the passengers with a goblet of hot, sweet coffee, laced with local whisky and topped with floating cream – and the beverage Irish coffee is born.

1976

Palestinian Liberation Organization (PLO) gunmen hijack an Air France flight at Tel Aviv airport and take the plane to Entebbe in Uganda where President Idi Amin welcomes it on the runway. In retaliation for the subsequent liberating raid by Israeli commandos, Amin personally orders the murder of the seventy-five-year-old British-born Israeli hostage Dora Bloch, who is in a hospital in Kampala after being released by the hijackers due to her ill health, and the murder of hundreds of Kenyans living in Uganda for Kenya's role in assisting Israel in the raid.

28
JUNE

1914

Having already failed this morning to kill the Austrian Archduke Franz Ferdinand in Sarajevo, Yugoslav nationalist student Gavrilo Princip is standing by a side-street café when the royal car, lost in the maze of streets, reverses and stalls outside the café. Princip shoots both the Archduke and his wife, Sophie, beginning a chain of events that will lead to the onset of the First World War.

1919

Five years to the day of the shooting of Franz Ferdinand, the First World War is formally ended by the signing of the Treaty of Versailles, which will itself sow the seeds of the Second World War.

1987

For the first time in history, a purely civilian target is subjected to a gas attack when Iraqi bombers ambush the Kurdish town of Sardasht in the country's northern reaches. Apart from the immediate casualties, 25 per cent of the population continues to suffer from severe illness and other medical problems resulting from the attacks.

1988

The longest trial in Spanish history, over contaminated olive oil, comes to a close after fifteen months. The epidemic caused more than 600 deaths and thousands more were partially paralyzed.

29
JUNE

1613

The original Globe Theatre in London burns down. During a performance of Shakespeare's *Henry VIII*, a cannon is fired to lend dramatic impact to the entrance of the character playing the king but it also manages to set fire to the thatched roof and rafters. The only casualty is a man whose breeches catch fire.

1801

The first census in Britain records a population of 8,800,000.

1914

Russian mystic and advisor to the Romanov Imperial family, Rasputin, is visiting his hometown of Pokrovskoye, Siberia, when Jina Guseva tries to assassinate him. She stabs him in the lower abdomen, purportedly claiming 'I have killed the Antichrist!' – but he knocks her to the ground. The injury will leave him in constant and considerable pain until his actual murder two years later.

1956

With the press proclaiming them 'the most unlikely couple since the Owl and the Pussycat', American actress Marilyn Monroe and playwright Arthur Miller marry in London today.

1995

In the first joint space venture of its kind, the American shuttle *Atlantis* docks with the Soviet Mir space station. The Americans bring chocolate and fruit and are given a traditional Russian welcome of salt and bread.

1520

Having murdered the Aztec Emperor Montezuma II, Spanish conquistador Cortés and his men have to fight their way out of the city of Tenochtitlan during the Spanish conquest of Mexico. Gastrointestinal infection suffered by travellers to the region will forever after be known as Montezuma's Revenge.

1908

The Tunguska Event occurs in Siberia today, involving a major explosion that knocks down some 80 million trees across an area of about 800 square miles (2,150 km²). The cause of the explosion will be argued for decades but the most likely estimate of the blast's energy is more than 1,000 times stronger than the atomic bomb dropped on Hiroshima.

1934

The start of the infamous Night of the Long Knives, during which German Chancellor Adolf Hitler purges the Nazi Party of elements he believes have grown too powerful. The name predates the Nazi assassinations and is taken from a fifth-century treacherous massacre of British Celts by Germanic Saxons known for their proficiency with the seax, or long knife.

1997

British Colonial rule in Hong Kong ends as the city is handed over to China.

1
JULY

1874

The Sholes & Glidden typewriter goes on sale with the Qwerty keyboard, as invented by American Christopher Latham Sholes. Contrary to myth, the layout does not slow typists down, but speeds them up by separating frequently paired letters that would otherwise get jammed together.

1916

First day of the Battle of the Somme in the First World War. British troops are told to advance to mop up after artillery has smashed the German emplacements. But the Germans have dug in deep and are largely untouched. Strolling over no-man's-land as if off to a garden party, the British are mown down in their thousands; on this day alone Allied casualties number 65,000 with a mere 8,000 on the German side. All told, the Somme will claim 500,000 or more from each side.

1943

Tokyo City is absorbed into the Tokyo Prefecture which comprises twenty-three wards. Strictly speaking, from today Tokyo ceases to exist as a city.

1962

After 132 years of French rule, the last eight locked in a bitter revolution, Algeria votes on the Independence Referendum proposed by French President Charles de Gaulle. The result is a landslide for separation.

2

1776

The American Congress votes through the Declaration of Independence, with John Adams proclaiming the date to stand in history as the founding of America in freedom. Nobody actually signs anything on 4 July, which was instead the date the printers finished the broadsheet versions for publication and so dated their work.

1853

Russia invades Moldavia and Wallachia, sparking the Crimean War.

1881

American President James A. Garfield is shot by unstable would-be statesman Charles Guiteau in Baltimore, and dies in September of his wounds. Guiteau will be hanged in the following June.

1900

The first Zeppelin, the LZ 1, takes to the air over Lake Constance on the Rhine in southern Germany.

1950

The beautiful Zen Buddhist Temple of the Golden Pavilion in the ancient Japanese capital of Kyoto is burned down by a schizophrenic novice monk, Hayashi Yoken, who then tries to burn himself alive but fails. A replica will be completed in 1955.

3
JULY

1844

The last Great Auk in the British Isles is killed by three fishermen on St Kilda who think the strange bird is a witch.

1884

Dow Jones publishes its first stock report.

1940

More than 1,200 French sailors die when the British Navy attacks their fleet at Mers-el-Kébir, Algeria. France has fallen to Nazi Germany and the action aims to prevent French ships falling into German hands. Incensed, two days later the French Air Force bombs the British fleet at anchor in Gibraltar.

1969

The original leader and founder of the Rolling Stones, English rock musician Brian Jones is found dead in his swimming pool at Cotchford Farm in Sussex, the house where A.A. Milne wrote *Winnie the Pooh*.

1987

Klaus Barbie is found guilty of war crimes at a court in Lyon, France. SS Commander of the city during the Second World War, he had earned the epithet of the Butcher of Lyon but after the War American intelligence agents spirited him away to work for their anti-Communist efforts. Hidden in Bolivia, in 1967 Barbie probably helped the CIA capture the Argentine guerilla Che Guevara.

4
JULY

1826

On the supposed anniversary of the American Declaration of Independence (in fact, the vote for independence had been taken on 2 July 1776 instead) two of the prime movers of that event, Thomas Jefferson and John Adams, die within hours of each other.

1862

To keep the 10-year-old Alice Liddell amused on a boating trip in Oxford, the English mathematician Charles Dodgson (Lewis Carroll) tells her a fantastical tale of a little girl in an underworld adventure that will become *Alice's Adventures in Wonderland*. The Liddells will soon take steps to keep the author away from their daughter as they are allegedly concerned about his obsessive attentions to her.

1934

The first woman to lecture at the Sorbonne, the first woman to win a Nobel Prize and one of only four people to be afforded that accolade twice, the Polish-born scientist Marie Curie dies in France.

1946

The Philippines gains independence from the United States.

2009

The crown of the Statue of Liberty is reopened to the public after being closed as part of post-9/11 security measures in New York, USA.

5
JULY

1841

Thomas Cook, a leading English Temperance preacher hires a train to take his congregation on a round trip from Leicester to Loughborough to hear other tub-thumpers railing against the Demon Drink. Cook realizes there is money to be made in such ventures and he is soon organizing grander excursions.

1865

The 'Red Flag Act' is passed in the UK restricting all steam-powered vehicles to 2 mph (3.2 kph) in urban areas and requiring them to be preceded by a man waving a red flag.

1937

Noted later as a term for unwanted e-mails, the meat product Spam goes on the market. The only country in which Spam is no joking matter is Hawaii, where they hold Spam-fests to discover new and interesting ways of presenting the stuff – so much so that in mainland USA Spam is widely known as Hawaiian steak.

1945

Having led the country through the Second World War, British Prime Minister Winston Churchill is swept out of office by a Labour election landslide. Ironically, this is the result of so many servicemen returning home, determined that things have got to change. King George VI offers him the Order of the Garter but Churchill declines, saying that he is content with the Order of the Boot given him by the people.

6

JULY

1809

Disgruntled at having been excommunicated by Pope Pius VII, Napoleon Bonaparte annexes the Papal States and lays siege to the Vatican, having the pontiff dragged from his bed and arrested. He will be imprisoned in Savona until released in 1814 by Allied troops who return him to the Vatican.

1885

Not being a qualified doctor, the French inventor of pasteurization Louis Pasteur risks prison by testing his rabies vaccine on nine-year-old Joseph Meister. The boy survives and stays in the Pasteur Institute in Paris as a janitor until, in 1940, he commits suicide after thinking – wrongly – that his family have been killed in the German invasion. Tragically, they return home one hour too late to save him.

1944

Future baseball star Jackie Robinson challenges the American military over racism. The military buses are meant to be non-segregated but Robinson, an army lieutenant, is told by a bus driver to move to the back seats for 'coloureds'. He refuses and is arrested by military police. At the subsequent court-martial he is acquitted by a panel of nine white officers.

1988

The North Sea oil platform, Piper Alpha, explodes in a fireball that claims 167 lives. Firefighting legend Red Adair will be brought in to deal with the blaze.

7
JULY

1853

In a classic example of gunboat diplomacy, American Commodore Matthew Perry approaches Edo Harbour with a fleet of warships to open negotiations on American-Japanese trade. He is eventually successful, gaining the Japanese title of Taikun, or Great Lord. Given the commercial nature of his venture, this is interpreted at home as 'tycoon'.

1937

The Second Sino-Japanese War starts and, later this year, will feature the infamous Rape of Nanking when Japanese troops run amok. About 300,000 Chinese are killed with an unknown incidence of rape and sexual murder. China will have to wait until 19 January 2013 for any form of apology from Japan.

1941

Although not yet involved in the Second World War, American troops occupy neutral Iceland, relieving the British occupying force. Iceland hopes that the presence of another neutral country will make it a less likely target for German bombers. After the attack on Pearl Harbor in the coming December, that will become irrelevant.

2005

Fifty-two people are killed and a further 700 injured in co-ordinated suicide-bombings on the Underground and on a bus in London. Tapes sent to Al Jazeera TV state the attacks are in retaliation for the British military presence in Iraq and Afghanistan.

8
JULY

1099

The First Crusade captures Jerusalem and begins to slaughter the population and loot the city.

1889

The last bare-knuckle world title boxing match is staged in Richburg, Mississippi, USA. After an incredible seventy-five rounds, John L. Sullivan finally knocks out Jake Kilrain. All subsequent official matches will be fought with gloves under the Queensberry Rules.

1892

On 29 June, Francisca Rojas had run bloody and screaming from her house outside Buenos Aires in Argentina to claim her neighbour had attacked her and killed her children. After interrogating the neighbour, Police Inspector Eduardo Alvarez doubts his guilt and returns to the house to try something he has heard about – fingerprinting. He finds a bloody smear which can be identified, and Rojas herself becomes the first person convicted of a crime on such evidence alone.

1982

Iraqi President Saddam Hussein escapes an assassination attempt in Dujail, central Iraq. In retaliation, hundreds of people are arrested, many are tortured, and about 160 are executed, including some children. In addition, thousands of acres of croplands around the town are razed to the ground to prevent other gunmen finding cover. These killings are one of the primary charges for which Saddam will hang in 2006.

9
JULY

1922

The Romanian-Austro-Hungarian-American swimmer Johnny Weissmuller breaks the one-minute barrier by swimming 100 metres (328 feet) in 58.6 seconds. Almost ten years later to the day he signs with MGM to play the lead in the first of countless *Tarzan* movies.

1943

According to legend, the American invasion of Sicily during the Second World War is assisted by the Mafia. On the promise of release after the War, Italian-American mobster Lucky Luciano has phoned Sicilian capo Don Vizzini to organize local support for the invasion force. Once established in Sicily, the Americans' 'liaison officer' is none other than gangster Vito Genovese.

1951

American crime-writer Dashiell Hammett, author of *The Maltese Falcon*, is asked in a district court to name communists in the film world. He refuses, taking the Fifth Amendment, and is thrown into jail. He is later blacklisted by Senator McCarthy's House Committee on Un-American Activities.

1958

The world's highest recorded mega-tsunami rips through Lituya Bay in Alaska following an earthquake in Gilbert Inlet at the head of the bay. The sea-bound tsunami peaks at a height of 1,720 feet (524 m) and reaches speeds of over 120 mph (193 kph). Fortunately it is soon dissipated when it hits the ocean.

10
JULY

1099

The Spanish Christian hero El Cid dies in the besieged city of Valencia. It is myth that he orders his body be dressed in armour and strapped onto his horse to lead a charge out of the city to break the siege and, despite Charlton Heston's depiction of him on film as a devout Christian warrior, he spent most of his time fighting as a Moorish mercenary.

1962

A multinational initiative, the communication satellite Telstar is launched, relaying the first television broadcasts the next day.

1976

A weedkiller factory outside Meda, Italy, springs a leak and envelops the town and environs in a toxic cloud of dioxins. More than 80,000 local farm animals have to be slaughtered to prevent them entering the food chain and the effect on wildlife and water supplies is incalculable.

1985

Tired of environmental activist organization Greenpeace interfering with its nuclear tests in the Pacific, France sends agents to blow up the Greenpeace ship *Rainbow Warrior* in Auckland, New Zealand, killing a crew member. Two French agents will be captured and charged, but after France formally apologizes they are transferred into French custody and soon released.

11
JULY

1893

Having left school at the age of thirteen to sell vegetables to the pearl divers of Ise in Japan, Mikimoto Kokichi develops the first-ever cultured pearls. To the chagrin of his previous customers, he soon becomes a multimillionaire.

1975

Chinese archaeologists uncover the 'Terracotta Army', thousands of sculptures of soldiers and horses belonging to the subterranean tomb of the First Emperor of China. The tomb had been discovered on 29 March 1974 by three farmers digging for water in Shaanxi province.

1977

In a landmark decision, the British magazine *Gay News* is fined £1,000 after being found guilty of blasphemy for publishing a poem intimating that Jesus was homosexual.

1979

Launched in 1976 by the US National Aeronautics and Space Administration (NASA), the space station Skylab crashes back to earth after a malfunction.

1995

Having overwhelmed the Dutch United Nations Peacekeeping Forces safeguarding Srebrenica in Bosnia, the Bosnian Serb Army takes over that supposed safe haven and slaughters more than 8,000 Bosnian Muslims who had gone there seeking sanctuary.

12
JULY

1191

The Third Crusade captures the city of Acre. Arab leader Saladin later offers surrender terms but King Richard I of England feels this is a delaying tactic, so he executes about 3,000 Muslim men, women and children.

1804

Mortally wounded yesterday in a dual with Vice-President Aaron Burr, the US Secretary of State Alexander Hamilton dies of his injuries.

1910

Charles Stewart Rolls, co-founder of Rolls-Royce cars, becomes the first British aviation victim when he crashes his Wright bi-plane near Bournemouth. The first person to fly across the English Channel and back non-stop, he is just thirty-two at the time of his death.

1971

The Australian Aborigines' National Flag is flown for the first time with official stature. Although most people use the word 'Aborigine' exclusively for natives of Australia, this is not quite correct since the term can apply to anyone there at the beginning – *ab origine*. The first people to be called Aborigines were the Latini (Latins) of Central Italy who became the Romans.

13
JULY

1793

Claiming to have information about traitors, French moderate Charlotte Corday visits Jean-Paul Marat, one of the leading radicals of the French Revolution, who is lying in his bath to alleviate his unpleasant skin condition. Corday cures this with a carving knife through his chest. She is connected to modern fashion bad-boy Jean Paul Gaultier through her mother, Charlotte Gaultier de Mesnival.

1814

Supposedly taking their name from the dung-beetle since they remove the bodies of plague victims from the cities, the military police force the Carabinieri is formed in Italy. Originally light mounted mercenaries, they are also famed for their short rifles, or carbines.

1837

Queen Victoria makes Buckingham Palace the prime royal residence. A few years later the palace is enlarged and its grand gateway has to be removed. Renamed Marble Arch, it is re-located to the old execution-ground of Tyburn that once stood west of the City of London, which supposedly gave rise to criminals talking of absent friends having 'gone west'.

1955

Ruth Ellis becomes the last woman to be hanged in the UK, for the murder of her two-timing lover David Blakeley.

14
JULY

1789

In one of the first acts of the French Revolution, a Parisian mob storms the Bastille fortress-prison to free its handful of prisoners and seize ammunition.

1881

'Wild West' outlaw Billy the Kid is shot to death by lawman Pat Garrett in New Mexico. Despite the Paul Newman 'bio-pic' *The Left-Handed Gun*, the Kid was right-handed but the first reproduction of a famous photograph of him reversed the negative.

1902

The famous Campanile of St Mark's Basilica in Venice, Italy, collapses just as the safety-inspection crew arrive for the annual check. Miraculously, the only casualty as the bell tower falls to the ground is the caretaker's cat.

1965

Mariner IV transmits the first pictures of the surface of Mars during its fly-by of the planet. It shows vast craters and red, sandy wastelands and evidence of other ancient, natural waterways.

2006

Poland becomes the only country in history to be governed by identical twins when Jaroslaw Kaczynski takes office as prime minister, having been nominated by his twin brother, President Lech Kaczynski.

15
JULY

1815

The Napoleonic Wars end when, deciding that the British are a safer bet than the Austrians or the Prussians, Napoleon surrenders himself to the captain of HMS *Bellerophon*.

1834

After 355 years, the Spanish Inquisition disbands. Contrary to popular myth, the Inquisition was not extreme, since it only tortured 2 per cent of suspects and only executed about a dozen per year. In contrast, in one ten-year period alone, other European countries dispatched more than 150,000 heretics and witches.

1954

Modelled on the long-range bombers the company produced throughout the Second World War, the Boeing 367-80 passenger airliner makes its maiden flight from Renton Field outside Seattle, USA. It goes into production as the iconic Boeing 707.

1997

Italian fashion designer Gianni Versace is shot and killed outside his Miami mansion by Andrew Cunanan, a gay prostitute who shoots himself as police close in on him on 24 July. No one will ever know why he did it.

16
JULY

1918

Having been held prisoner at Yekaterinburg, the Russian royal family and their doctor and servants are murdered. The drunken execution squad steal valuables from them before disposing of the bodies in acid-pits or down disused mineshafts.

1945

The US Army conducts the first nuclear test at White Sands in New Mexico. There are radial mile-markers so the devastation can be graded with the bomb at the centre, marked Ground Zero – the first use of the term. After the successful detonation, scientist Robert Oppenheimer is thought to have quoted from the Hindu *Bhagavad Gita*: 'Now I am become Death, the destroyer of worlds.'

1965

The Mont Blanc Tunnel opens, linking France and Italy.

1994

The comet Shoemaker-Levy 9 smashes into Jupiter at about 135,000 mph (214,000 kph), causing massive waves to race across the surface of the stricken planet.

1999

Not the luckiest of families, John F. Kennedy Jr, his wife Carolyn and her sister are all killed when the plane he is piloting crashes off the coast of Martha's Vineyard in Massachusetts, USA, not far from Chappaquiddick, scene of another Kennedy disaster.

17
JULY

1717

British King George I is taking an excursion in the royal barge on the River Thames when he finds himself pursued by another boat carrying musicians who offer him the premiere of composer George Handel's *Water Music*.

1871

American lawyer and Ohio state legislator Clement Vallandigham is in Lebanon, Ohio, to defend a man charged with murder during a barroom brawl. Vallandigham contends that the victim had gut-shot himself while trying to draw his gun from a crouched position. To demonstrate, he produces a pistol, crouches down and accidentally discharges the gun when trying to draw it from his pocket. Vallandigham dies but the jury is convinced and acquits his client.

1917

During the First World War, British King George V decides it is impolitic for the royal family to sport Germanic names such as Saxe-Coburg and Gotha. The raids made on London by Gotha bombers have made his mind up for him. The royal family becomes the Windsors, the Battenbergs become the Mountbattens, German shepherd dogs become Alsatians and dachshunds become sausage-dogs.

18
JULY

64

The Great Fire of Rome. Although Emperor Nero is accused of 'fiddling while Rome burns', the violin is not yet invented. He blames Christians for starting the blaze and afterwards persecutes them relentlessly.

1762

The feckless Russian Tsar Peter III is strangled by conspirators determined to put his wife, Catherine the Great, on the throne.

1870

The Vatican proclaims the Dogma of Papal Infallibility which does not mean the pope can do no wrong. Instead, it means that, when speaking *Ex Cathedra* (seated on the papal throne) and pronouncing on points of morals or faith, his word cannot be questioned.

1969

US Senator Edward Kennedy and political worker Mary Jo Kopechne slip away from a political party on Chappaquiddick Island, off the coast of Martha's Vineyard, at about 11pm, ostensibly for him to drive her home. He drives off a bridge and the car ends up upside down in the river. Kennedy gets out but Mary Jo dies.

19
JULY

1545

During the Battle of the Solent against French invaders, the pride of English King Henry VIII's fleet, the *Mary Rose*, sinks with the loss of about 750 lives. The wreck lies untouched until salvaged in 1982.

1799

In Egypt, a French officer of Napoleon's invasion force uncovers the Rosetta Stone, which carries the same text in Egyptian hieroglyphs, Demotic and Ancient Greek. It is the key to deciphering the hieroglyphics that have puzzled archaeologists for so long.

1821

British King George IV is crowned in Westminster while his estranged wife, Caroline of Brunswick, is barred from attending the ceremony. Some people argue that his marriage to Caroline is actually bigamous and invalid, since he had previously married in secret (although illegally) his real love, Maria Fitzherbert.

2001

British author and leading member of the political Conservative Party, Jeffrey Archer is sentenced to four years for perjury and perverting the course of justice. Back in 1986, the *Daily Star* newspaper had accused him of paying a prostitute for sex, an allegation he denied, winning £500,000 damages. He is found to have lied over this denial, and apart from the jail term he is also ordered to repay the damages along with the £1.3 million legal fees incurred by the newspaper.

20
JULY

1944

German leader Adolf Hitler is left injured but survives after Lieutenant Colonel Count von Stauffenberg's bomb plot narrowly misses its target at Rastenburg, East Prussia. In the savage aftermath of the failed assassination, of the 7,000 arrested 4,980 will be executed, including Field Marshal Erwin Rommel who is forced to take poison.

1951

King Abdullah of Jordon is assassinated at the Al-Aqsa Mosque in Jerusalem by a Palestinian gunman who fears Jordan will make peace with Israel. Abdullah's grandson Hussein is also shot, but is saved by a medal he is wearing which deflects the bullet.

1969

Having announced today from the moon that 'The Eagle has landed', American astronaut Neil Armstrong will tomorrow step out of the capsule to declare: 'That is one small step for a man, one giant leap for mankind'.

1974

Turkey invades Northern Cyprus.

1984

The man who started the jogging craze, Jim Fixx, dies of a heart attack while out jogging.

21
JULY

1796

Scottish bard Robert Burns dies in Dumfries at the age of thirty-seven. Although widely credited with writing the popular New Year's Eve song 'Auld Lang Syne', he recorded that he copied it down after hearing an old man singing it.

1973

Agents of the Israeli intelligence unit Mossad, hunting the Munich Olympics killers, shoot and kill innocent Moroccan waiter Ahmed Bouchiki in Lillehammer, Norway, in a case of mistaken identity. Mossad will repeat its folly in Beirut in 1979 by killing four passers-by and injuring another eighteen when agents car-bomb their true target.

1988

After eight years of attrition, the Iran-Iraq War ends with Iran's Ayatollah Khomeini announcing he is prepared, reluctantly, to accept the UN Security Council's Resolution 598 that lays out terms for the ceasefire. By now, nearly three million are dead or injured and millions more are homeless.

2005

Just two weeks after the 7 July bombings in London, four terrorist devices fail to explode on the Underground with only the detonators going off. In the frantic response, the following day innocent Brazilian Jean Charles de Menezes is gunned down on the Underground by police firing hollow-point rounds that leave him unrecognizable.

22
JULY

1934

Anna Sage, a Romanian prostitute threatened with deportation, goes on a cinema-date with American gangster John Dillinger. But, the day before, she had struck a deal with the FBI to 'finger' Dillinger in return for bounty money and the right to remain in the US. She wears an orange dress (red in popular legend) for ease of identification and, when the cinema empties out, Dillinger is gunned down. The FBI gives Sage just $5,000 and further reneges on the deal by allowing her to be deported anyway.

1991

Serial killer Jeffrey Dahmer is arrested in Milwaukee after Police discover human remains in his apartment. He will be convicted of the murder of sixteen men and boys and on other charges including rape, necrophilia and cannibalism. He will only serve two years of his life sentence before being beaten to death by a fellow inmate.

2011

Having bombed a government building in Oslo, Norwegian right-wing extremist Anders Breivik, dressed as a policeman, wanders into a youth camp on the island of Utoya and kills sixty-nine people, mainly teenagers, and injures many more. He will be sentenced to twenty-one years with the option to extend that sentence by blocks of five years.

23
JULY

1745

Bonnie Prince Charlie (Charles Edward Stuart) lands on the Outer Hebrides Isle of Eriskay to launch the Second Jacobite Rebellion against British King George I. The prince has been raised in Italy and cannot understand the Scottish islanders, who are not expecting him and almost kill him on the beach.

1858

The Oath of Allegiance is modified in Britain to allow Jews to take office in parliament.

1929

In a move that will be followed by France in the 1980s and again in 2008, Italian dictator Benito Mussolini bans the use of foreign words in print or broadcasts throughout Italy.

1942

The Nazis open their extermination camp outside Treblinka in Poland. Operating until a revolt and breakout in 1943, the camp sees the murders of more than 1 million people, who are originally buried in huge pits. The bodies will be dug up and burned when the Nazis realize mass graves leave clear evidence of atrocities.

1951

Marshal Philippe Pétain, leader of the collaborating French Vichy government during the Second World War, dies in prison, serving a life sentence, aged 95.

24
JULY

1701

The French trapper, trader and explorer, Antoine de Cadillac, establishes a trading post in North America which will evolve into the city of Detroit. The Detroit-built famous limousine cars are – much later – named in his honour.

1847

Mormon leader Brigham Young founds Salt Lake City in Utah. In 1855, the Mormons establish the satellite settlement of Las Vegas, where Mormon banks are later involved in setting up brothels and casinos.

1943

During the Second World War, the Allies launch Operation Gomorrah, the week-long, systematic and relentless bombing of the important industrial port of Hamburg. The resultant tornado-like firestorm will produce winds of 150 mph (240 kph) that suck people in as temperatures reach 1,400° F (760° C). Some 50,000 people die and parts of the city are vaporized.

1950

A modified captured German V2 is the first rocket to be launched from what is at this stage a tiny installation at Cape Canaveral in Florida, chosen for its proximity to the equator, where the earth's rotational speed is greatest.

25
JULY

1587

Christianity is outlawed in Japan and Jesuit missionaries are expelled.

1917

Margaretha Zelle, aka Mata Hari, is found guilty of spying for Germany and will face the firing squad in October. Although perceived as a woman of vampish beauty, she is by now a portly forty-one-year-old, showing all the signs of alcohol, drugs and syphilis.

1978

Louise Brown, the world's first 'test-tube' baby is born in England.

2000

Just two minutes after take-off from Charles de Gaulle airport near Paris, an Air France Concorde falls out of the sky and onto a small hotel in the town of Gonesse. All 109 on board are killed, as are four on the ground.

2009

The oldest surviving veteran of the First World War trenches, Englishman Harry Patch, dies aged 111, one month and one day. This almost echoes the conflict's end on the eleventh hour of the eleventh day of the eleventh month of 1918.

26
JULY

1908
The US Attorney General Charles Joseph Bonaparte – whose family is connected to French Emperor Napoleon Bonaparte – founds the forerunner of the FBI, the Office of the Chief Examiner.

1936
The Axis powers of Germany and Italy announce that they will intervene in the Spanish Civil War, giving General Franco the air power he needs to win the conflict.

1952
Eva Perón dies. Eight people die in the crowds that gather in mourning around the presidential residence and 2,000 require hospital treatment for crush injuries.

1953
Cuban revolutionary Fidel Castro mounts his first attempt at a coup with his failed raid on the Moncada Barracks. He is captured and imprisoned.

1956
Within weeks of taking power, President Nasser of Egypt nationalizes the Suez Canal, bringing his country into conflict with Britain, France and Israel.

2004
Project Frozen Ark is launched in Britain to store the DNA of all endangered species.

27
JULY

1794

One of the architects of the Reign of Terror following the French Revolution, Maximilian Robespierre is himself arrested and will be guillotined the next day. He had coined the word 'terrorism' to describe draconian measures employed by the State; not until the late twentieth century will it be applied to 'freelance' activists.

1953

After the loss of more than a million lives, the Korean War is finally brought to a close.

1976

Former Japanese Prime Minister Kakuei Tanaka is arrested for taking bribes from the American Lockheed Corporation in return for allowing Nippon Airlines to buy Lockheed passenger planes.

1980

The exiled Shah of Iran dies in Egypt, praying on his deathbed for the overthrow of the Ayatollah Khomeini.

2003

Two months after his hundredth birthday, American comedian Bob Hope dies. He never won an Oscar and, when hosting the 1968 Awards, he said: 'Welcome to the Academy Awards. Or as it is known in my house – Passover.'

28
JULY

1655

The French dramatist and duelist Cyrano de Bergerac dies aged only thirty-five.

1945

In thick fog an American military B-25 bomber plane crashes into the Empire State Building in New York, killing the crew and fourteen others. Lift operator Betty Lou Oliver's elevator plunges down seventy-five floors, but the reams of severed lift cable below it form a bouncy steel cushion, helping her to survive.

1945

With America demanding the immediate unconditional surrender of Japan towards the end of the Second World War, Japanese Prime Minister Kantaro Suzuki replies with an unfortunately ambiguous word variously translated as 'we have not yet decided' or 'no comment' or even 'ignore'. It is interpreted as this last meaning, so atomic bombs are dropped on Hiroshima and Nagasaki.

1976

The devastating magnitude 7.5 Tangshan earthquake in China claims perhaps 655,000 lives. It is a major coal-mining centre and, with the night shifts fully manned when the quake strikes, no one makes it back to the surface.

29
JULY

1588

The Spanish invasion fleet the Armada is sighted off England. According to legend, the English Admiral Sir Francis Drake decides to finish his game of bowls before attending to the invasion. In fact Drake, the English second-in-command, is already on his ship ready for battle. The invasion eventually fails.

1890

Suffering from depression, Dutch painter Vincent van Gogh dies two days after shooting himself at Auvers in France.

1907

Having conducted a trial camp on Brownsea Island off the Dorset coast of England, British Army officer Robert Baden-Powell announces the formation of the Boy Scouts organization.

1966

American singer Bob Dylan claims that he has broken several vertebrae in a motorcycle accident near Woodstock. But since no ambulance is called and there is no record of his having been hospitalized, many people believe this is his cover story for withdrawing from touring for eight years.

1981

More than 700 million people worldwide watch the marriage of British Prince Charles to Lady Diana Spencer broadcast from St Paul's Cathedral, London.

30

1864

The Battle of the Crater during the American Civil War: Union forces have besieged the Confederates at Petersburg and, to break the stalemate, Union General Ambrose Burnside decides to dig a tunnel up to the walls and blast it open. But the blasted trench or crater leaves his charging men trapped to be shot like fish in a barrel. Nearly 4,000 Union men – many from African-American troops – are killed, wounded or captured.

1966

England wins the football (soccer) World Cup for the first time since its inception in 1930.

1975

Controversial American Union boss Jimmy Hoffa disappears from the parking lot of the Machus Red Fox restaurant in Bloomfield, Detroit, never to be seen again. He will be legally declared dead on this same day in 1982, thus fuelling the myth that persons missing for seven years can be automatically declared legally dead.

1978

Having endured the post-War chaos of changing the road systems to driving on the right to suit the American Occupation Force, the Prefecture of Okinawa in Japan today reverts to the old system of driving on the left, with another round of chaos and traffic accidents.

31
JULY

1910

The first criminal to be caught by radio telegram, American homeopath Dr Crippen is arrested when the ship he is fleeing Britain on docks in Canada. The ship's captain had become suspicious about Crippen's mistress, Ethel le Neve, travelling disguised as a boy, and sent a message that was passed to Scotland Yard. Crippen will hang for the murder of his wife.

1964

American singer 'Gentleman Jim' Reeves crashes his private plane in a storm near Nashville, Tennessee, killing himself and his passenger, his manager Dean Manuel.

1970

'Black Tot Day' sees the final issue of rum in the British Royal Navy. A tradition dating back centuries, the original issue was half a pint per man per day of rum, reduced in 1824 to a 'tot' or two-and-a-half ounces. This was in addition to rations of beer, which stored better than water on long voyages.

1991

START, the Strategic Arms Reduction Treaty, is signed by Presidents George Bush of the USA and Mikhail Gorbachev of the Soviet Union. It reduces each side's nuclear weapons by 35 per cent and is the first military agreement between the superpowers since the 1970s. The Soviet Union collapses before the treaty is implemented, but the Russian Federation and three other former Soviet states later ratify it.

1
AUGUST

1774

British chemist Joseph Priestley publishes his 'discovery' of oxygen. Although he takes the credit, he has only replicated the 1773 experiments of the Swede Carl Scheele, known as Hard-Luck Scheele for his kudos being usurped by others.

1834

The Slavery Abolition Act of 1833 comes into force in the British Empire. In reality, only slaves aged six or under will get their freedom; those over six will have to continue as 'apprentices' until 1 August 1840 as the Government does not have enough money to compensate all slave-owners at once.

1966

Ex-Marine Charles Whitman barricades himself into a building at the University of Texas and starts sniping indiscriminately. He kills sixteen before being shot by police.

1984

A prehistoric body is dug up by peat-cutters working on Lindow Moss just outside Wilmslow, Cheshire. In 1983, the partial remains of a female had been found but this body, christened Pete Marsh, is a major archaeological find – his body is almost complete and he had been ritualistically killed.

2

AUGUST

1100

English King William II (Rufus) is 'accidentally' killed by an arrow fired by one of his own entourage while hunting in the New Forest. The hit-man, Walter Tirel flees for France as William's younger brother Henry loots the Treasury and declares himself king.

1870

Tower Subway, an underground railway, opens in London between Tower Hill and Vine Lane on the south bank. It later gains notoriety when it is suspected that Jack the Ripper, whose 'playground' lies in nearby Whitechapel, is using the network of maintenance tunnels as escape routes.

1876

'Wild Bill' Hickok is shot in the back as he plays poker in a saloon in Deadwood (now in South Dakota). He is holding a pair of aces and a pair of eights, a combination now known as the Dead Man's Hand.

1943

US Navy motor torpedo boat *PT-109* is rammed and sunk by the Japanese destroyer *Amagiri*, propelling its commander, Lt John F. Kennedy, to the role of war-hero after he saves several of his crew.

1990

Saddam Hussein of Iraq precipitates the Gulf War by invading Kuwait.

3

216BC

Rome is left counting the cost of yesterday's clash with Hannibal of Carthage at the Battle of Cannae, south-east Italy. The most devastating defeat in its history, the Roman Army lost about 56,000 men to an enemy who lost a mere 6,000.

1492

Christopher Columbus embarks from Spain on the expedition that will see him land in the New World. It is his first voyage in the now-famous *Santa Maria*.

1921

The first aerial crop dusting is conducted on a farm in Troy, Ohio, to rid the owner of a plague of caterpillars.

1926

The UK's first traffic lights are installed at London's Piccadilly Circus.

2003

The American Anglican Community invites hostility from conservative elements at home and abroad by voting to appoint the first openly gay bishop, Gene Robinson. The divorced father-of-two has been living openly with his partner for more than fourteen years.

4
AUGUST

1693

Today, according to French legend, the Benedictine monk Dom Pérignon invents champagne. But, in 1632 Christopher Merrett, a cider-maker of Gloucester, England, had delivered a paper to the Royal Society detailing his process for instigating secondary fermentation in French wines. Could champagne be an English invention?

1704

Britain captures Gibraltar from Spain. Always of prime strategic importance, the island had been used by the Saracen warlord Tariq as his base for the invasion of Spain in 711. He called the island Mount of Tariq or 'Jebel Tariq'.

1914

After Germany refuses to withdraw its troops from Belgium, Britain enters the First World War with the press proclaiming that it will all be over by Christmas.

1944

Following a tip-off from an unidentified informer, the Gestapo discover a secret annex attached to a warehouse in Amsterdam and arrest Anne Frank, her family and four other Jews hiding from Nazi persecution. All but Anne's father will die in concentration camps.

5

AUGUST

1305

The Scottish national hero William 'Braveheart' Wallace is captured by the English and taken to London for execution as a traitor, although he claims he had never offered allegiance to the English throne. The film *Braveheart* shows the Scots in tartan plaids, but these were not worn then; the Scots and the English of the day dressed much the same.

1884

The cornerstone of the Statue of Liberty is laid. A gift from France to the United States, it is designed by architect Frédéric Auguste Bartholdi.

1944

The last banzai charge of the Second World War is made by Japanese prisoners in the Australian POW camp at Cowra, New South Wales. More than 1,000 inmates charge the fence and gun towers, resulting in 235 deaths before the situation is brought under control. The word 'banzai' is based on a Chinese phrase meaning, rather ironically, 'may you live forever'.

1962

Film star Marilyn Monroe is found dead next to an empty bottle of Nembutal sleeping pills. Pathologist Dr Thomas Noguchi will later state that no trace of the capsules or the drug are evident in her intestines, indicating that she had not *swallowed* the fatal dose. A conspiracy theory arises that her death was arranged to prevent her going public about her affair with President John F. Kennedy.

6
AUGUST

1890

The electric chair is used for the first time to dispatch murderer William Kemmler in New York, USA. All does not go to plan; it takes two attempts with Kemmler almost on fire at the end of an eight-minute ordeal, leaving witness and inventor George Westinghouse to comment that they would have done better with an axe.

1914

Although German Zeppelins have dropped the odd bomb or two before, today sees the first planned, formal air raid: Liège in Belgium is bombed, killing nine people. Air raids on London begin on 31 May 1915 and continue until September 1916, when the advent of incendiary ammunition renders the airship too vulnerable to fly in combat.

1945

The Enola Gay, an American bomber named after its pilot's mother, drops the first atomic bomb on Hiroshima, Japan. Although badly burned, survivor Tsutomu Yamaguchi makes his way home to Nagasaki and is discussing his experiences with his boss on 9 August when he sees a terrifyingly familiar flash in the sky, signalling the Americans' second atomic bomb. Yamaguchi survives and will die on 4 January 2010, aged 94.

1991

British scientist Tim Berners-Lee opens the World Wide Web by posting files on a newsgroup about its ethos and function.

7

AUGUST

1782

American President George Washington institutes the Badge of Military Merit – the forerunner of the Purple Heart – for those heroically wounded or killed in the War of Independence. There are only three recipients, after which the award lapses from use until revived in 1932 by General Douglas MacArthur.

1840

There will be no more children up chimneys after today's vote in the British Parliament bans the use of such 'apprentices' to chimney sweeps, most of whom keep the boys thin by starving them. The suggestion to adopt the French method of dragging a tethered and panicking goose backwards down the chimney on a line is met with disapproval.

1913

Samuel Cody, an American aviator who created man-lifting kites for military observation, becomes the UK's first air fatality when he crashes his new plane at Farnborough. His kite and balloon unit will evolve into Number One Squadron of the Royal Flying Corps and will retain that status when the Corps becomes the Royal Air Force.

1972

Branding them bloodsuckers, Ugandan President Idi Amin announces the country's 60,000 Asians have ninety days to leave or face the death penalty. Amin has already begun moves to confiscate their homes and businesses and freeze bank accounts.

8
AUGUST

1576

As the Danish mathematician and astronomer Tycho Brahe lays the cornerstone for the world's first observatory at Uraniborg his nose falls off. In 1566 he had fought a duel – in a darkened room – over the validity of a mathematical equation and lost his nose in the farce. For the rest of his life Brahe had to wear a metal replacement nose – plain copper on working days with a more ornate silver-and-gold one for nights out.

1844

Following the lynching of Mormon leader Joseph Smith in Illinois, the Mormon Church elects Brigham Young as his successor. He bans African-Americans from the priesthood and instigates posthumous Mormon baptism of the dead. Jewish people will later be outraged by the Mormon baptism of victims of the Holocaust and of Adolf Hitler.

1929

The German airship, the *Graf Zeppelin*, sets out on its round-the-world flight.

1945

Hot on the heels of the Hiroshima bombing, a Russian force is racing towards Hungnam in Korea to confiscate everything and everyone working on the Japanese atomic bomb programme that has already conducted successful tests. What they capture brings the Soviet bomb programme forward by about twenty years.

9
AUGUST

1930

Originally drawn as an anthropomorphic French poodle, the character Betty Boop makes her debut in a cartoon entitled *Dizzy Dishes*.

1942

Mahatma Gandhi is arrested in Bombay, India, for demanding that Britain should 'Quit India'. Already alarmed by nationalist Subhas Chandra Bose, who has raised an army of 100,000 to fight for Germany against the Allies, the British finally realize they are no longer welcome in India and will set in motion their withdrawal after the Second World War.

1945

The second atomic bomb is dropped on Nagasaki, Japan. The original target town Kokura was scratched at the last minute due to poor visibility. Kokura is indeed a lucky town – it was the secondary target for the first atomic bomb if poor conditions had prevailed over Hiroshima.

10
AUGUST

1775

Having seized Acadia in French Canada, the British begin the deportation of all Acadians who will not swear allegiance to the British Crown. Thousands are transported to the other end of North America and dumped in New Orleans.

1793

The Louvre opens as a modest affair with about 600 objects on display. It will evolve into the world's most visited museum with nearly ten million visitors tramping its miles of galleries every year.

1966

The last man executed in Oklahoma, USA, before the suspension of capital punishment between 1972 and 1976 – James French – goes to the electric chair with the headline: 'French Fries'.

1984

American golden-girl Mary Decker crashes out of the Helsinki Olympic Games 3,000-metres-race after clashing with barefoot runner Zola Budd, the South African athlete hurriedly given citizenship by the UK so she could compete under the Union Jack. Budd is initially disqualified but later the panel of judges rule that Decker's aggressive move to pass was the cause of her fall.

1988

US President Ronald Reagan reluctantly authorizes compensation to American citizens of Japanese descent who were illegally interned during the Second World War.

11
AUGUST

3114BC

The commencement date of the Mayan Long Calendar. Because it ends on 21 December 2012, many New Agers decide that this will be the end of the world, but the prophecy does not come true and we are still all here.

1921

American writer Alex Haley is born. He will become known for his epic saga *Roots*, which purports to trace his family roots back to the African slave, Kunta Kinte, taken from the Gambia. But in 1978 District Court Judge Robert J. Ward will rule the book a 'hoax' and order compensation paid to Harold Courlander, author of *The African*, the novel Haley plundered for ideas.

1956

The almost permanently drunk Amerian artist Jackson Pollock crashes his car, killing himself and passenger Edith Metzger. His mistress, the twenty-six-year-old Ruth Kligman, is thrown clear and survives. Pollock is forty-four.

1965

Twenty-one-year-old African-American Marquette Frye is arrested for drunk-driving in the Watts neighbourhood of Los Angeles. The ensuring scuffle escalates into the Watts Riots, lasting six days. Frye never collects his car since the impound fees exceed its value.

12

30BC

Cleopatra VII of Egypt commits suicide, possibly not with an asp but by taking poison. Having had a love affair with Julius Caesar of Rome, she later married Caesar's friend Mark Antony and fought in vain with him against Caesar's nephew Octavian (Emperor Augustus). She is the last pharaoh of Egypt.

1822

The British Foreign Secretary, Lord Castlereagh slits his throat with his penknife, possibly to avert exposure in a homosexual scandal or perhaps because of depression. His nephew, Robert FitzRoy, the man who will captain HMS *Beagle* to the Galapagos Islands and take along the twenty-two-year-old Charles Darwin as a travelling companion, will likewise dispatch himself with a razor in 1865.

1908

The first Model T car rolls off the Ford production line to revolutionize motoring. Nicknamed the Tin Lizzie, Henry Ford's automobiles are the first generally affordable cars, and will gain such a reputation for reliability that gangsters Clyde Barrow and John Dillinger will both write to him saying there is no better getaway car on the market. The letters are in the Ford Museum but the company, perhaps wisely, will decide against using them for advertizing.

13
AUGUST

1860

Phoebe Ann Moses, better known as sharpshooter Annie Oakley, is born in rural Ohio, USA. Although she certainly was a crack shot, much of her pistol and rifle ammunition had been converted to mini-shotgun load to make it easier to hit balloons and other targets from a moving horse.

1863

Jostled off the platform at New Jersey Station and into the path of a train, a young man is dragged back to safety by another commuter. The man in danger is Richard Todd Lincoln, son of US President Abraham Lincoln, and his saviour is well-known actor Edwin Booth, the brother of John Wilkes Booth who, two years later, will assassinate the president.

1914

Having been laid-off from his job as a driller at the 3M's iron-mining operations in Hibbing, Minnesota, American Carl Wickman starts a bus service out to his old place of employment. His buses, like everything else in the area, get coated in grey dust from the mines, so his passengers will nickname this new and speedy service the Greyhound, the name Wickman uses for his bus company today.

14
AUGUST

1893

The first compulsory car registration plates are introduced in France.

1900

The 55-day siege of the foreign legations in Beijing (Peking), China, is broken, effectively ending the Boxer Rebellion. Before sending in his troops, Kaiser Wilhelm II of Germany tells them to act without mercy, just like Attila the Hun. His address ensures that 'Hun' will be used in future as an epithet for any German.

1908

The first international beauty contest is held at the Folkestone Hippodrome in Kent, UK, attracting entrants from France, Italy, Spain, Germany and Denmark. The winner is English contestant Nellie Jarman, and the front two rows in the auditorium are taken up by suffragettes who wave banners throughout.

1917

China enters the First World War, declaring war on Germany and Austria.

1945

With the Japanese emperor about to announce surrender at the end of the Second World War, a contingent of senior army officers attempt a military coup in what is known as the Kyujo Incident.

15
AUGUST

1040

Scottish nobleman Macbeth kills King Duncan of Scotland and takes the throne. On this same date in 1057 he will himself be killed by Malcolm, son of Duncan.

1914

Upset at being called a 'black son-of-a-bitch' by draughtsman Emil Brodelle, gardener and cook Julian Carlton wreaks his revenge at architect Frank Lloyd Wright's commune/work-complex at Taliesin in Wisconsin, USA. He kills Wright's mistress, Mamah Borthwick, and her two children, then sets the place ablaze and stands by with an axe to attack any who make it out of the building, killing seven.

1947

The Union Jack is lowered for the last time in India and the Hindu-Muslim bloodbath begins.

1969

The Woodstock Festival opens on Max Yasgur's farm near Bethel, New York. Remembered by some as a spontaneous concert organized by hippies, it was instead a calculated venture by a consortium of entrepreneurs who told Yasgur to expect 5,000 attendees and pay him $10,000 for the rental of his land. Nearly 500,000 turned up (tickets cost $125 at modern values although most get in for free) but the post-festival lawsuits for damages will leave the 'suits' of Woodstock Ventures paying out twice what they had made.

16

AUGUST

1819

Large crowds have gathered at St Peter's Field, Manchester, England, to demand parliamentary reforms. Local officials, becoming nervous, summon the cavalry, who are, according to one report, roaring drunk. They charge the crowd causing eleven deaths in what will be known as the Peterloo Massacre.

1858

The first messages are sent down the newly completed Transatlantic Cable. Unfortunately, electricians attempt to strengthen the signal by firing very high voltages down the line but only manage to fry the cable.

1888

Thomas Edward Lawrence is born in Wales. In the film based on his experiences as a British Army officer, *Lawrence of Arabia*, he is shown leading his 'camelry' in a glorious charge to wrest the city of Aqaba from the grip of the Turkish Army. In fact, before the battle, whooping and firing his revolver wildly, he manages to shoot his own camel in the head and has to be rescued.

1960

US air force officer Joseph Kittinger free-falls from a balloon sailing about 19 miles (31 km) over New Mexico to set a record for the highest skydive. It stands unbroken until 14 October 2012 when Austrian Joseph Baumgartner repeats the stunt over the same state from a height of 23 miles (37 km). Baumgartner also breaks the sound barrier.

17
AUGUST

1585

English colonists sent under charter by Sir Walter Raleigh arrive on Roanoke Island, North Carolina, to establish what is usually claimed to be the first European settlement of North America. But Vikings under Leif Eriksson, some time around the year 1000, had established a base in Newfoundland, Canada.

1786

US politician Davy Crockett is born in Tennessee. Hollywood would later give him the coonskin hat and buckskins he never wore: he never hunted bears; he never roamed the frontier; he couldn't hit the side of a barn when shooting and his legend will end when he dies at the Battle of the Alamo, in 1836.

1962

Although a few others have died in various attempts to escape East Berlin, eighteen-year-old Peter Fechter today becomes the first to be shot by East German border guards at the Berlin Wall. In 1997 two guards will be convicted of Fechter's manslaughter, and East German leader Egon Krenz will himself be sentenced to six years in prison for instigating the shoot-to-kill policy on the Wall.

2005

As part of Israel's Plan of Disengagement from the West Bank, the army begins the enforced evacuation of Jewish settlements. The settlers, previously encouraged to go there by the same government, put up considerable resistance and will subsequently be collectively awarded over $200 million in compensation.

18
AUGUST

1227

Genghis Khan dies, aged perhaps 65. Although some scholars use his name as a byword for brutality, he was less draconian than the ancient Romans, and he is still revered in Mongolia and China.

1503

Pope Alexander VI dies after a dinner party. Better known as Rodrigo Borgia, he has perhaps accidentally drunk some of the poisoned wine he has prepared for his host. Poisoning is so common in Italy that the cautious insist on tipping wine from their goblet into that of their host. Suppposedly this ritual develops into the clinking of goblets before a toast.

1587

Virginia Dare is the first English child born in the New World. Her parents are part of the original English settlement on Roanoke Island, North Carolina but what becomes of her is unknown as all settlers will disappear.

1899

Lucy Gaston founds the Anti-Cigarette League of America in Chicago. By 1907 she will have persuaded the Illinois legislature to ban the manufacture or sale of cigarettes, although this will be overturned by the Supreme Court. Adolf Hitler will be the first to pass modern anti-smoking legislation, with bans on smoking in public transport, public buildings and restaurants in Germany.

19
AUGUST

1895

One of the genuine gunslingers of the so-called Wild West, John Wesley Hardin, who by his own admission killed 42 men, is himself gunned down at the dice-table of a saloon in El Paso, Texas. Not taking any chances, outlaw-turned-lawman John Selman, with whom Hardin had been arguing, walks in and shoots the gunman in the back of the head.

1942

Of the 6,083 men who take part in today's disastrous Allied raid on Dieppe, more than 60 per cent fail to return. Two days earlier, *The Telegraph* newspaper crossword leads with a clue to which the answer is Dieppe, but an investigation finds nothing but coincidence. By another coincidence, the compiler is none other than Leonard Dawe – see 6 June.

1960

US pilot Gary Powers is sentenced to ten years in a Soviet jail after his U-2 spy-plane has been shot down over the USSR.

1977

American comedian Julius 'Groucho' Marx dies. His nickname possibly deriving from the fact that he could be pretty grouchy, he was constantly under scrutiny by the FBI who suspected him of communism. His legacy endures: for example rock band Queen named albums after his films – *A Night at the Opera* and *A Day at the Races.*

20
AUGUST

1619

The first African slaves are brought to the Jamestown settlement in Virginia by Dutch traders. But not all slaves in seventeeth-century America are black; in 1676 the Virginia State Legislature will pass laws prohibiting free blacks from owning white slaves or even hiring white servants.

1924

As depicted in the film *Chariots of Fire*, Scottish runner Eric Liddell withdraws from the 100-metre race in the Paris Olympics since the qualifying heats are being run today, which is a Sunday, and to do so would be against his religious beliefs.

1940

Backed by a joint KGB-Gestapo team, Soviet agent Ramón Mercader, a Spaniard, wheedles his way into Leon Trotsky's compound in Coyoacán near Mexico City, and plants an ice axe into the exiled Russian revolutionary's head. Also implicated in the assassination are artists Diego Rivera and his wife, Frida Kahlo.

1968

Growing tired of the 'Prague Spring' demands for political liberalization in Czechoslovakia, Soviet troops (and those from its Warsaw Pact allies) invade the country. Former child film star, Shirley Temple, who has become an American diplomat and has only recently arrived in Czechoslovakia, is forced to hurriedly depart. She will return as US ambassador to a free Czechoslovakia in 1989.

21

AUGUST

1759

Étienne de Silhouette, Finance Minister of France, announces the cuts he deems necessary to avert national bankruptcy. Soon 'on the Silhouette' comes to mean anything on the cheap – especially the new craze for low-priced, black-outline portraits.

1879

Fifteen people witness the alleged appearance of the Virgin Mary, St Joseph and St John the Evangelist at the church in Knock, County Mayo, Ireland.

1911

There is panic in Parisian art museum the Louvre when it is noticed that the Mona Lisa is no longer hanging on the wall. Museum employee Vincenzo Peruggia has simply walked out with the painting he deems stolen from his home country – Italy – by Napoleon Bonaparte. Artist Pablo Picasso is one of the people dragged in to the police enquiry as a suspect.

1986

Lake Nyos in Cameroon explodes. Sitting above a chamber of carbon dioxide, Nyos has been absorbing the gas to saturation point. Tonight an earth tremor shakes the lake like a giant fizzy drink bottle, allowing it to disgorge as much as 1.6 million tons (2,300 kg) of gas in one almighty belch. Three thousand cattle and 1,700 people living about the shores are suffocated immediately and others drown in the huge tsunami that follows.

22
AUGUST

1485

The last and decisive battle of the Wars of the Roses is fought on Bosworth Field, England, where Henry Tudor (later King Henry VII) is victorious over King Richard III, the last of the Plantagenet dynasty. Richard's ancestors had adopted the name Plantagenet from the Latin name of the common broom shrub, indicating they will sweep everything away before them.

1654

Jacob Barsimson, the first Jew to settle in America, arrives in what will become New York. Within days his back-up party of twenty-three also arrive to found what will become a thriving Jewish community. Come the twentieth century it contains more Orthodox Jews than live in the whole of Israel.

1902

Born today, German photographer Leni Riefenstahl will film the growth and 'triumphs' of the Third Reich. After the Second World War she will be shunned by the movie community but will collaborate with sci-fi writer L. Ron Hubbard, founder of Scientology.

1953

The last prisoners on Devil's Island are released as France hands over the tiny island near French Guiana to its National Centre for Space Studies for monitoring rocket launches.

23
AUGUST

79

After grumbling for a few days, Mount Vesuvius in Italy erupts to engulf the cities of Pompeii and Herculaneum in searing hot gas and volcanic dust.

1382

The Golden Horde of the Mongols lays siege to Moscow, eventually conquering the city. The term 'Golden' might lie in the nomadic warriors' origins in the Crimean Peninsula, a land formation known in their language as an 'or', which term becomes confused with the French word for gold.

1839

Britain captures Hong Kong from the Chinese.

1914

The first major clash of the First World War takes place as the Allies engage the Germans on the first day of the Battle of Mons.

1939

Germany and the USSR sign a non-aggression pact.

1973

Swedish bank-robber Jan-Erik Olsson becomes trapped inside a Stockholm bank with four hostages. Over the next few days these five forge a bizarre psychological bond with the hostages conniving to thwart police moves to free them. This phenomenon is later studied by psychiatrists who call it the Stockholm Syndrome.

24
AUGUST

1185

Normans from the Kingdom of Sicily capture the city of Thessalonica (in modern Greece) as part of their conflict with the Byzantine Empire.

1542

Gaspar de Carvajal, a member of a Spanish expedition along a mighty South American river, records encounters with naked female warriors along its banks. This is thought to be the origin of the name of Amazon, although an alternative explanation is that it derives from a local name for the river – Amassona, the boat-destroyer.

1608

The first English traders land at Surat, marking the beginning of the British presence in India. On the same date in 1690, Job Charnock of the East India Company founds the city of Calcutta (Kolkata) with his trading post.

1770

Having been exposed as a forger and a plagiarist, the seventeen-year-old would-be poet Thomas Chatterton takes arsenic. His tragic, youthful death revives interest in his work, and he finally gains fame, if only posthumously.

2006

The Astronomical Union today strips Pluto of its status as a planet.

25

AUGUST

1900

Friedrich Nietzsche, the German philosopher so dear to the Nazi party, dies.

1925

The Brotherhood of Sleeping Car Porters union is formed in America. Members want better working conditions, and to end the practice of African-American porters being called 'George' by rail-travellers. George Pullman's sleeping car company's adverts advising travellers to 'Sit back and let George do it' have been so successful that not only do travellers scream out 'George' to attract attention but the new autopilot systems have also attracted the nickname.

1942

British King George VI's younger brother, the Duke of Kent, dies with fourteen others when their plane crashes into a hill in Scotland. Although his destination is a mystery, he is the first member of the royal family to die on active service in more than 500 years.

1944

Towards the end of the Second World War the liberation of Paris is complete. With the city's loss, Adolf Hitler demands that landmark buildings should be blown up before German forces withdraw, but whether he could not or did not want to, the German Military Governor of the city, General Dietrich von Choltitz, surrenders without destroying Paris.

26
AUGUST

55BC

Roman leader Julius Caesar attempts his first invasion of the land of the Pritannes, a tribe his spies have wrongly told him is called Britannes. As a result he erroneously names their country 'Britain'.

1346

The French and English armies engage today at Crécy in northern France where the longbow helps win the day for the English army. Actually, the weapon is of Welsh invention and, with English yew too knotty to make a good bow, most longbows have been imported from Europe. The vast majority of 'English' bows are made of Iberian yew.

1676

Born today, Sir Robert Walpole will later be erroneously hailed the first prime minister of Great Britain. The official title of Prime Minister for the leader of the British Government will not exist until the opening of the twentieth century, making Henry Campbell-Bannerman the first so recognized. Almost all previous incumbents held the office of First Lord of the Treasury.

1883

The Indonesian volcano Krakatau (Krakatoa) erupts, killing more than 36,000. It is the loudest explosion in history, audible 1,930 miles away (3,110 km) with its sound waves recorded on barographs round the globe.

27

AUGUST

1913

Russian pilot Pyotr Nesterov is the first to fly a plane through a complete loop.

1955

The arbiter in many a bet and argument, the first edition of the Guinness Book of Records is published. Four years before, Sir Hugh Beaver, the Chairman of Guinness Brewery, was discussing which game bird was the swiftest, and, as he could find no book of such records, he commissioned journalists Norris and Ross McWhirter to produce one.

1967

Brian Epstein, manager of the Beatles, dies of a drugs overdose. Discharged from the Army for dressing as an officer, he was addicted to alcohol and gambling. Speculation surrounds his cloistered 1963 holiday in Spain with John Lennon, who once assaulted DJ Bob Wooler for even suggesting a liaison had taken place.

1975

The deposed emperor of Ethiopia, Haile Selassie dies in Addis Ababa. He is the focal point of the Rastafari movement.

1981

Protestors begin a march from Cardiff to the US airbase at Greenham Common, UK. It is the beginning of the Women's Peace Camp objecting to the presence of cruise missiles.

28
AUGUST

1898

Having tested the market with what he called Brad's Drink, American drugstore owner Caleb Bradham relaunches his blend as Pepsi-Cola. He will go bankrupt in 1923 and sell out to a consortium of investors for $35,000. Time will prove that a canny investment.

1955

The murder of 14-year-old African-American Emmett Till in Mississippi will act as a catalyst for the Civil Rights Movement. Visiting from Chicago, Till is deemed guilty of 'reckless eyeballing', or looking at white women. His attackers gouge out one of the teenager's eyes before shooting him and flinging the body off the Tallahatchie Bridge of *Ode to Billie Joe* fame.

1957

Senator Strom Thurmond makes the longest filibustering speech in American political history. Trying to delay the vote on the Civil Rights Act, he talks for twenty-four hours and eighteen minutes. His discrimination towards African Americans did not prevent him, at the age of twenty-two, from impregnating the sixteen-year-old family maid, Carrie Butler, who was promptly fired in accordance with old Southern values.

2005

Hurricane Katrina reaches peak strength in the early hours and goes on to wreak catastrophe on the city of New Orleans. At least 1,833 people die.

29
AUGUST

1918
For the first time, the British police go on strike for higher pay.

1949
The USSR detonates its first test nuclear bomb.

1950
The first detachment of British troops – 4,000 personnel – arrives in Korea for what will prove a long and costly war.

1966
The Beatles play their last concert in their last American tour at Candlestick Park, San Francisco. In the wake of John Lennon's announcement that the Beatles are more popular than Jesus, the band was met at Memphis, Tennessee, by the Ku Klux Klan holding a burning cross with a Beatles album nailed to it.

1986
Beating the odds of about 700 million to one, Britain's oldest twins, May and Marjorie Chavasse, turn 100 years old with four generations of their family attending the birthday celebrations.

30
AUGUST

1918

Russian political activist Fanny Kaplan attempts to assassinate Lenin. She is arrested and is summarily executed within days. One of her bullets lodges in Lenin's neck; four years later, doctors will try to remove it, triggering the series of strokes that will kill him. However, the bullet removed is not from the gun that Kaplan was alleged to have been carrying, and as she was half-blind, she would have been a very poor assassin! Some modern historians believe the assassination story was made up to justify Lenin's crackdown on dissent.

1980

After shipyard workers go on strike, Poland becomes the first Eastern Bloc country to officially give workers the right to strike and the right to independent trade unions. A couple of weeks later the Solidarity trade union is formed, led by Lech Walesa.

1988

Loaded with toxic waste originating in Italy, the West German freighter, the *Karin B*, is today anchored off Plymouth, England, after being turned away from every port in Europe. She had first unloaded in Nigeria but even the bribes offered were not enough to prevent the ship being reloaded and sent packing.

Eventually, she will have no option but to return to Italy.

31
AUGUST

1422

Henry V dies while on campaign in France leaving his son, the nine-month-old Henry VI, to assume the throne as the youngest monarch in the history of England.

1857

British Army officer Sam Browne loses his left arm at Seerporah in India. No longer able to steady his scabbard as he draws sabre, he designs a wide leather belt, supported by a diagonal shoulder strap, to carry his pistol-holster. The Sam Browne belt will be worn by everyone from Adolf Hitler to Canadian Mounties.

1869

The first road traffic victim is Irish scientist Mary Ward who falls from the car in which she was travelling and rolls back under its wheels.

1888

The body of Mary Nichols is found in Bucks Row in London's Whitechapel; a well-known prostitute, she is the first confirmed victim of Jack the Ripper.

1997

British Princess Diana and her companion Dodi al Fayed are killed in a car crash in a Paris tunnel. Conspiracy theorists will become obsessed by the suggestion that the couple are assassination victims, but it appears that their driver, Henri Paul, was drunk.

1
SEPTEMBER

1894

The Great Hinkley Fire in Minnesota, USA, lays waste to up to 200,000 acres (809 sq km) and kills possibly 800 people. Among the dead is Boston Corbett, the soldier who, contrary to orders, shot John Wilkes Booth, the assassin of Abraham Lincoln.

1958

The First Cod War starts when Iceland declares an exclusion zone of 12 nautical miles (22.2 km) about its shores

1969

Colonel Muammar Gaddafi seizes power in Libya.

1974

USAF Majors James Sullivan and Noel Widdifield set the so-far unbroken record time for a New York-London flight of one hour and fifty-four minutes.

1983

Korean airliner Flight 007 strays into prohibited Soviet airspace and is shot down killing all 269 on board. The Kremlin insists that the liner was also a spy-plane.

2004

Chechen separatists take over the main school in Beslan, Northern Russia, holding more than 1,000 children and staff hostage. On 3 September Soviet forces will storm the complex, resulting in the deaths of 334 hostages.

2

SEPTEMBER

1666

The Great Fire of London begins, consuming vast tracts of the city but only causing six known deaths. London's population is about 500,000 but when the Great Plague came in 1665 perhaps two-thirds of these fled the city.

1898

On a mission to re-conquer the Sudan, British General Sir Herbert Kitchener leads an army of 25,000, equipped with the new Maxim machine guns, to confront the 50,000-strong Sudanese Dervish force at Omdurman. Some 10,000 Dervishes are killed in the first assault with a further 13,000 wounded; Kitchener loses forty-seven men. Young Winston Churchill, riding with the 21st Lancers, is shocked at the execution of the wounded.

1945

Japan signs the formal surrender document at the end of the Second World War. During the American occupation of the country cosmetic breast surgery comes to Japan. With Americans preferring the fuller figure, petite Japanese prostitutes turn to surgeons who realize silicone is the answer.

1973

English author and academic J.R.R. Tolkien dies. During one of the meetings of the Inklings literary group in Oxford when he was reading from his then-unpublished work *The Lord of the Rings*, Shakespearean professor Hugo Dyson exclaimed, 'Oh God! Not another fucking elf!' before walking out.

3

SEPTEMBER

1189

The coronation of King Richard I of England at Westminster. He does not speak English and will spend less than ten months of his short life in the country. He will die on the parapets of the castle of Châlus-Chabrol in France, taunting attacking bowmen, one of whom gets in a lucky shot.

1833

The *New York Sun* is launched as the first half-sized newspaper, intended to be easier to read on crowded trams and trains. The first paper to call itself a 'tabloid', the *Westminster Gazette*, will later be sued by pharmaceutical firm Burroughs, Welcome & Co for infringement of its registered trade name for the compressed pills called 'tabloids'.

1939

Britain declares war on Germany. Within hours the passenger ship SS *Athenia* is sunk off Rockall by a U-boat. The 117 who die will become the first British, Canadian and American casualties of the Second World War.

1967

Sweden shifts to driving on the right. At 4:50 am in the morning, traffic comes to a halt then swaps sides, moving off again at 5:00 am. The first-ever speed limits are imposed to reduce accidents and, although unpopular, will remain in place.

4
SEPTEMBER

1965
The German-French Lutheran doctor and missionary Albert Schweitzer dies in the Gabon where he has spent most of his life.

1978
Severe flooding in northern India means that about two million people become homeless.

1985
Explorer Robert Ballard releases the first pictures of the wreck of RMS *Titanic* on which more than 1,500 people died in 1912. Lying two-and-a-half miles below the surface (four km), the wreck has been filmed by his robot-sub Argo. Plans by others to salvage or even raise the liner bring protests from those who deem the site a grave that should be left in peace, especially *Titanic* survivor Millvina Dean who will oppose any such moves until her death on 31 May 2009.

1989
Georges Simenon, the Belgian creator of detective Jules Maigret, dies leaving a suspect legacy. Thought to be a Nazi collaborator, he was tried on camera in France in 1950 and banned from publishing anything for five years, a punishment kept from the public. He claimed to have slept with 10,000 women, which questions how he found the time to write more than 200 books and short works.

5

SEPTEMBER

1921

Movie star Roscoe 'Fatty' Arbuckle hosts a party during which actress Virginia Rappe is fatally injured and dies two days later. The media speculate that she has been sexually molested, and Arbuckle will face three trials for rape and accidental manslaughter. Although he is eventually cleared his career is finished.

1972

Palestinian terrorists break into the Olympic village in Munich, West Germany and attack Israeli athletes. Two Israelis die immediately and nine are held hostage with the gunmen demanding the release of over 200 Palestinian prisoners held in Israel as well as safe passage out of Germany. In the shoot-out following a rescue attempt, five of the gunmen, one German policeman and all the hostages die.

1980

The 10½-mile-long (16.9 km) Gotthard Tunnel between Göschenen and Airolo in Switzerland opens. The 2001 fire in the tunnel will be approached with what appears to be reluctance and excessive caution, just as with the 1999 Mont Blanc Tunnel fire. But perhaps the firemen know what the public don't – allegedly every bridge and tunnel in the country has been wired for demolition in case of foreign invasion.

6
SEPTEMBER

1901

After today's assassination of US President William McKinley by Leon Czolgosz at the Pan-American Exposition in Buffalo, Robert Todd Lincoln, son of Abraham and there in Buffalo at the president's invitation, decides not to attend any further presidential events. He should have been present at his father's death; he was present when President Garfield was shot in 1881, and now feels he might be something of a jinx.

1941

Wrongly believing it a symbol of ancient significance to all Jews, the Nazis today make it law for Jews to wear a yellow Star of David badge. In fact it is barely fifty years since the symbol was officially adopted by the First Zionist Congress of Prague in 1897. Prior to this it was more of an esoteric religious symbol.

1944

The scene of so much slaughter in the First World War, Ypres is the first major town in Belgium to be liberated by the Allies on their push towards Berlin.

1966

The South African architect of apartheid, Prime Minister Hendrik Frensch Verwoerd, is assassinated.

1997

The funeral of Diana, Princess of Wales takes place in Britain with more than two billion people watching around the world.

7
SEPTEMBER

1812

French Emperor Napoleon Bonaparte defeats the Russian army at Boridino, 60 miles (96 km) west of Moscow, and then makes the fatal mistake of pressing on to that city from which he will have to withdraw under onslaught from the greatest of all Russian generals – Winter! Hitler will make the same mistake.

1838

The steamship *Forfarshire* founders near the Longstone Lighthouse off the coast of Northumberland, England. Grace Darling, daughter of the lighthouse-keeper, becomes famous for helping rescue survivors.

1978

Georgi Markov, a Bulgarian dissident, is walking across Waterloo Bridge in London when he is shot in the leg with a ricin pellet fired from an umbrella-gun, probably by Bulgarian agent Francesco Gullino.

1986

Already a Nobel Peace Prize-winner, human rights activist Desmond Tutu is enthroned as Archbishop of the South African Anglican Community, making him the spiritual leader of over two million and thus a political force to be reckoned with.

8

SEPTEMBER

1504

A masterpiece by Italian artist Michelangelo, the statue *David* is unveiled to the public at Florence's Palazzo Vecchio.

1886

Prospectors flock to White Waters' Edge, or Witwatersrand, in South Africa to dig up the gold to make coins that will be named from the last element of that toponym: 'rand'.

1943

The surrender of Italy in the Second World War is announced. On 3 September, Pietro Badoglio, prime minister since the ousting of Mussolini in July, had given an unconditional surrender to Allied commander General Eisenhower, while telling the Germans that Italy would fight on till the end. Today the truth is revealed, infuriating German leader Adolf Hitler.

1974

Just to tidy up history, US President Gerald Ford issues a pardon to the previous incumbent, Richard Nixon ('Tricky Dicky') for his role in the Watergate Scandal.

1979

Probably dead by her own hand since 30 August, the body of American actress Jean Seberg is found in the back of her car in Paris. Because of her support for the African-American activists the Black Panthers, the FBI had planted a false, scandalous story that she was pregnant by one of the Panthers' leaders.

9

SEPTEMBER

1585

Armand Jean du Plessis, the future Cardinal Richelieu, is born. He will become the Chief Minister of France and the original power-behind-the-throne, the colour of his red robes giving rise to his nickname of the Red Eminence, while his assistant, François Leclerc du Tremblay, will be nicknamed the Grey Eminence, giving rise to the term *éminence grise*.

1942

For the first time, the USA is bombed from the air when a Japanese floatplane, launched from a surfaced submarine, bombs Oregon in the first of several such missions on mainland America.

1975

While on tour in America, eighteen-year-old tennis player Martina Navratilova asks for political asylum. She has recently been told by her Czech 'minders' that she needs 're-education' as she is becoming too Americanized.

1976

Chairman Mao of China dies. Perhaps his worst idea was the 1958 War on Sparrows, a bird he blamed for eating crops. By 1960 the bird had been virtually eradicated in China causing a famine that killed over 30 million. Sparrows do eat grain but they also eat locusts which, left free of such predation, ran riot, devouring everything in sight.

10
SEPTEMBER

1952

West Germany agrees to pay compensation to Israel for war time atrocities including the persecution of Jews under the Nazi regime, the confiscation of Jewish property, and slave labour of Jews.

1971

Retired Soviet Premier Nikita Khrushchev dies. He is particularly remembered in the West for his antics in 1960 when, getting into a heated debate in the United Nations either with Harold Macmillan of the UK or Lorenzo Sumulong of the Philippines, he banged his shoe on his desk.

1981

Spanish artist Pablo Picasso's painting *Guernica* is at last sent from New York to Spain. The artist had always insisted that the painting should only be shown in his homeland when it once again enjoyed democracy.

1989

Hungary opens its Austrian borders allowing thousands of East Germans to out-flank the Berlin Wall and walk round to West Berlin.

2008

The Large Hadron Collider, the world's largest particle collider, powers up for the first time, successfully circulating proton beams, only to shut down days later after an explosive gas-leak.

11
SEPTEMBER

1649
The siege of Drogheda in Ireland by English Parliamentarian Oliver Cromwell comes to a bloody close. About 3,500 die.

1792
In the early days of the French Revolution, the Royal Storehouse is looted and many crown jewels are stolen, including the French Blue, a massive diamond that is smuggled to London where it is bisected, the larger piece going to Henry Philip Hope. Thought to be cursed, the Hope Diamond will pass through many hands before ending up in the Smithsonian Natural History Museum in the US.

1973
In Chile a US-backed military coup overthrows the elected Marxist regime of Salvador Allende who dies in the Presidential Palace. Right-winger Augusto Pinochet becomes leader of the junta.

2001
Three hijacked airliners are flown into the Pentagon and the twin towers of the World Trade Center in New York in a terrorist attack that kills and maims over 9,000. A fourth hijacked plane crashes in Pennsylvania after the passengers fight back. The New York site is now a national monument christened Ground Zero, a term first used by the Manhattan Project developing atomic bombs during the Second World War.

12
SEPTEMBER

490BC

This is possibly the day that the Greeks and Persians clash at the Battle of Marathon. Legend will claim that the courier Pheidippides ran back to Athens with news of the Greek victory only to drop dead after his announcement. The event is the inspiration behind the modern marathon race.

1683

The Turkish siege of Vienna is lifted and perhaps the croissant is born. According to some, the crescent-shaped pastry is of Viennese origin as bakers celebrate the fall of the Turkish Crescent banners around the city.

1910

Alice Stebbins Wells becomes the world's first policewoman with full powers of arrest when she is sworn in by the Los Angeles Police Department in the USA.

1919

Adolf Hitler attends a meeting of and later joins the German Workers' Party, forerunner of the National Socialist German Workers' Party or Nazi Party. Only their political opponents will use the tag of Nazi, as that was a pet name for idiots.

1977

Black activist Steve Biko dies after six days of 'interrogation' by the South African police in Port Elizabeth.

13

SEPTEMBER

1656

Croatian mercenaries are presented at the court of Louis XIV to thank them for their contribution to French victories over the Habsburg Empire. The Croats' name for themselves is Hravat, and the most distinctive part of their uniform is a loose silk square tied about the neck. This is soon copied by French courtiers with the name of cravat.

1788

The US Constitutional Convention announces plans for the first presidential elections. Since the convention is meeting in New York City, that city is currently the Federal Capital.

1943

The Nationalist General Chiang Kai-shek becomes head of state of China.

1959

The Soviet Luna 2 probe becomes the first spacecraft to reach the Moon.

1980

The grizzly bear called Hercules, missing for nearly a month, is recaptured in the Outer Hebrides, Scotland. He had escaped from the set of an advert for Kleenex tissues. Having lost over 20 stone (127 kilos), Hercules tucks into 120 pints of milk (68 litres) and dozens of eggs.

14

SEPTEMBER

1321

Italian poet Dante Alighieri dies leaving his *Divine Comedy*, a term then given to any story that does not have a tragic ending.

1852

British general and politician the Duke of Wellington dies. The conqueror of Napoleon Bonaparte, he was not always popular in Britain, and his epithet of the Iron Duke came not from his stern resolve in battle but because he had to install iron shutters on his house in London to prevent the windows being broken by protestors.

1944

Destined for fame for hosting the European Council, Maastricht is the first town to be liberated in the Netherlands from German forces.

1982

Princess Grace of Monaco (actress Grace Kelly) is negotiating a serpentine road between Monaco and Nice when her car suddenly plunges off a hairpin bend. Her daughter Stéphanie survives but Grace will die tomorrow.

1987

A group of German hackers called the Data Travellers breach the systems at NASA and NATO missile installations and start a panic by messing around with the launch codes.

15
SEPTEMBER

1789

The American writer James Fenimore Cooper is born. He will find fame with his *The Last of the Mohicans*, film versions of which will erroneously cause that tribe's name to be given to the punk hairstyle. It is in fact the Iroquois Native Americans, who, fighting for the French, sport the central plume of hair, and are thus nicknamed *Huron*, French for 'brush-head'.

1830

British politician William Huskisson becomes the first person ever to be killed by a train. Attending the opening of the Liverpool and Manchester Railway, Huskisson is distracted by the presence of Waterloo hero the Duke of Wellington, and is run over by inventor George Stephenson in his Rocket.

1928

Designed and built in Britain by W. H. Richards for the Model Engineering Exhibition in London, the first-ever humanoid robot is put through its paces. The name comes from Karel Capek's 1921 play R.U.R. (Rossum's Universal Robots), with the word 'robot' deriving from the Czech for slave.

1935

Nazi Germany announces the Nuremberg Laws that ban marriages between Jews and non-Jews, and effectively deny German citizenship to Jews. The Reichstag also adopts the Swastika as a national emblem.

16

1908

The American car-manufacturing holding company General Motors is formed. Within two years it will incorporate firms such as Buick, Oldsmobile and Cadillac.

1959

The American corporation Xerox demonstrates, on a live television broadcast from New York, the first successful plain paper photocopier, the Xerox 914.

1963

Malaysia celebrates its independence from Britain.

1986

Nearly 200 black mine workers are killed in the Kinross Gold Mine, South Africa, when sparks from a welding gun ignite the plastic foam lining of the tunnels. Banned in other countries, this material puts out highly toxic fumes and the country's mining companies are roundly condemned for the hazardous conditions to which workers are routinely exposed.

1987

Seventy countries sign the Montreal Protocol agreeing to limit their output of industrial gases that are damaging the ozone layer. Ironically, the recommended shift from petrol to ethanol in cars generates ozone pollution at ground level to cause serious respiratory conditions.

17
SEPTEMBER

1683

Dutch microscope-maker Antonie van Leeuwenhoek reports his observations of bacteria.

1814

Held prisoner on a British warship during the attack on Baltimore's Fort McHenry during the War of 1812, Francis Scott Key was overcome with emotion the morning of 14 September when he saw the American flag still flying from the fort. Today he puts the finishing touches to his poem 'Defence of Fort McHenry', which will be renamed 'The Star Spangled Banner' and become the national anthem of the USA.

1916

German pilot Baron Manfred von Richthofen wins his first aerial combat in the skies over Cambrai, France.

1929

The British Occupation Force that has been in Germany for over ten years begins its withdrawal.

1983

Vanessa Williams becomes the first African-American woman to take the title of Miss America but has to stand down for runner-up Suzette Charles after *Penthouse* magazine publishes nude photos of her. Undaunted, Vanessa goes on to a successful singing and acting career.

18
SEPTEMBER

1864

The death of British army officer John Hanning Speke on 15 September is today ruled mischance since he accidentally shot himself while out shooting game in England. Speke discovered the source of the Nile and his bizarre writings hail the Tutsi ethnic group of Africa to be the descendants of the Biblical character Ham and therefore rightly superior to the Hutu people they already dominate. This will all explode in Rwanda in 1994.

1939

The Irish-American fascist William Joyce makes his first broadcast from within Germany. He is now known as Lord Haw-Haw, but that name was also given by *Daily Express* writer John Barrington to another Nazi propagandist called Norman Baillie-Stewart who did have a marked upper-class English twang.

1961

Swede Dag Hammarskjöld, Secretary-General of the United Nations, is killed along with his entourage when their plane crashes in what will become Zambia. He is there to negotiate a ceasefire between the factions of a bush war, but speculation begins that he has been assassinated.

1970

Iconic American electric guitarist Jimi Hendrix dies, probably of an accidental drugs overdose, in London, England.

19
SEPTEMBER

1356
Edward, the so-called Black Prince of England, vanquishes the French at the Battle of Poitiers during the Hundred Years' War.

1876
The American inventor Melville Reuben Bissell patents his carpet sweeper, which will not change in basic design for the next 120 years.

1893
New Zealand is the first country in the world to grant the unrestricted enfranchisement of women. In the same year, Elizabeth Yates is elected Mayor of Onehunga (now a suburb of Auckland) making her the first elected female official in the British Empire and possibly the world.

1905
Having helped thousands of destitute children into the group homes he founded in Britain, the philanthropic Irish-Italian Dr Thomas Bernardo dies.

1955
Argentine President Juan Perón is deposed in a military coup and goes into exile.

1985
An earthquake of 8.1-magnitude strikes near Mexico City, killing at least 10,000 people.

1519

Ferdinand Magellan sets out from Spain on the first successful circumnavigation of the world.

1863

Jacob, one of the Brothers Grimm, dies. Their raunchy and violent folk tales will be seriously bowdlerized to render them acceptable for children.

1870

During the Second War of Italian Independence, troops of the first unified Italian King Victor Emmanuel II advance on Rome where Pope Pius IX is exhorting his Swiss guards to prepare for action. But, as they are heavily outnumbered, they soon throw in the towel leaving the pope no option but to surrender. Rome becomes part of the Kingdom of Italy.

1970

The Soviet Luna 16 lands on the Moon and begins to gather rock-samples to be bought back to earth for examination.

1984

Islamic militant suicide bombers drive an explosive-laden truck into the compound of the American Embassy in Beirut, Lebanon, and detonate the load to kill 24 people.

21
SEPTEMBER

1327

English King Edward II is killed in Berkeley Castle in Gloucestershire.

1915

Having owned the monument since the early 1800s, the Antrobus family auction the ancient stone circle Stonehenge to Sir Cecil Chubb for £6,600. Parts of the prehistoric site in Wiltshire, England, can be dated to 3000BC, with some elements lining up with celestial bodies and thought to be marking the winter and summer solstices. However, no one knows who built Stonehenge nor why.

1955

Ignoring claims of ownership from both Denmark and Iceland, Britain today annexes the uninhabited and desolate island of Rockall in the Outer Hebrides to stop it being used by the Russians as an observation platform to spy on missile tests.

1989

With the law lagging behind surrogacy and frozen embryo technology, the Tennessee Supreme Court in the USA rules in favour of the divorced Mary Sue Davis, granting her custody of the seven fertilized and frozen pre-embryos stored by her and her husband in more harmonious times. Her ex, Junior Davis, has complained that he should not be forced to become a father against his will and then be presented with the bill for maintenance. He will later win his case on appeal.

1735

London newspapers announce that on the previous day Sir Robert Walpole, the British First Lord of the Treasury (Prime Minister) has moved into 10 Downing Street. The street is named after Sir George Downing, a miserly diplomat. The last private occupant of part of the new Number 10 was a Mr Chicken of whom nothing is known.

1828

Shaka Zulu, King of the Zulu, is murdered by his half-brothers. Shaka is credited with revolutionizing the Zulu fighting style by incorporating the short spear and tall shield and he also invented the devastating Buffalo Head attack in which the 'impi' or regiment would split into three with the central corps smashing into the enemy lines while the 'horns' encircled to attack the flanks.

1862

President Lincoln issues the Preliminary Emancipation Proclamation which, although famous, frees no one as it calls on the Confederate States over which he has no control to free *their* slaves.

1980

After weeks of cross-border spats, the Iran-Iraq War begins in earnest.

23
SEPTEMBER

45BC

Knowing he has not long to live, Roman dictator Julius Caesar files his will in Rome. He will die next March with many wrongly believing that the manner of his birth gave rise to the phrase 'caesarean' section. He did, however, impose his *Lex Caesarea* requiring all unborn infants to be cut from dead mothers for separate burial. Such an operation is known in German as the Kaiserschnitt, in Russian as the Tsar-cut, and in similar equivalents in many other languages as diverse as Hebrew and Korean.

951

German King and Holy Roman Emperor Otto the Great takes control of Italy. According to legend, he realizes the need to generate horse-power to control his ever-expanding empire, and establishes a breeding farm on the edge of the Black Forest. This will grow into the town of Stuttgart, or stud-farm, which explains the prancing horse on the badge of the Porsche cars made there.

1846

German astronomer Johann Gottfried Galle announces the existence of a large planet that is eventually named Neptune.

1870

Having begun on 19 September, the Prussian siege of Paris is now complete. By the time it is lifted next January, the Parisians will have eaten all the animals in the city, including the itinerary of the three zoos, and be down to the cats, rats and dogs.

24
SEPTEMBER

1877

The end of the samurai, or hereditary military nobility, in Japan. The Meiji Restoration of 1868 dismantled feudalism, leaving the shoguns (military governors) and samurai an anachronism. But in January some 40,000 samurai joined the Satsuma Rebellion that ends today with the Battle of Shiroyama where the last surviving forty samurai, armed only with swords, deliberately charge to their deaths against the musketry of the Imperial Forces.

1890

Faced with the threat of confiscation of temples and the revocation of civil rights of its members, the Mormon Church in the USA renounces polygamy.

1947

In the Hindu-Muslim bloodbath following the British withdrawal from India, a train crowded with Muslims fleeing to the newly established Pakistan is stopped by Sikhs who slaughter all 1,200 or more passengers.

1950

Massive forest fires in Canada begin to black out the sun.

1960

The world's first nuclear-powered aircraft carrier, the USS *Enterprise*, is launched in America. Its name will be adopted for the spacecraft in television series *Star Trek*.

25
SEPTEMBER

1780

His name to stand forever in America as a synonym for a traitor, General Benedict Arnold makes it clear that he has swapped sides in the War of Independence and is working for the British.

1932

The region of Catalonia takes autonomy from Spain, setting up its own parliament, designing its own flag and reverting to its own language.

1957

Federal troops fix bayonets to form a cordon and protect nine African-American students as they enrol at the previously all-white Central High School in Little Rock, Arkansas.

1959

Solomon Bandaranaike, Prime Minister of Sri Lanka, is shot by Buddhist monk Talduwe Somarama and will die of his injuries tomorrow. The victim has abolished the death sentence but Somarama, whose motives are never made clear, is hanged anyway.

1983

Thirty-eight Irish Republican prisoners escape from the Maze Prison near Lisburn in Northern Ireland, using a hijacked delivery truck to ram the main gates. This is the largest and most embarrassing breakout for the British authorities since 1974, when thirty-three inmates tunnelled out of the same complex.

26
SEPTEMBER

1687

With its name coming from the Greek for 'virgin' since it once housed unmarried women's apartments, the Parthenon temple on the Acropolis in Athens is reduced to ruins. Rather than decaying over time, it is blown up when it takes a direct hit from Venetians attacking the Turkish occupiers who are using it as a munitions store.

1934

The ocean liner *Queen Mary* is launched today in Scotland by the other Queen Mary, wife of British King George V. When shipping firm Cunard asked his permission to name the new ship after the nation's most illustrious queen, meaning his grandmother, Victoria, the king said that his wife would be most flattered – so *Queen Mary* it was.

1937

African-American blues singer Bessie Smith is injured in a car accident and bleeds to death in an ambulance. It is a myth that a hospital turns her away because of the colour bar in racist Mississippi.

1960

Some 70 million Americans follow the first-ever televised debate between presidential candidates. Proving the power of image, most who watch on TV think that John F. Kennedy had won, while the majority of those listening on radio give victory to Richard Nixon.

27
SEPTEMBER

1590
Pope Urban VII dies of malaria thirteen days after being elected, the shortest papal reign in history.

1822
French scholar Jean-François Champollion announces that he has deciphered the ancient Egyptian hieroglyphs inscribed on the Rosetta Stone.

1888
The Central News Agency in London receives a letter from a man claiming to be the killer of all the prostitutes in Whitechapel. It is signed Jack the Ripper, the first time the name is used, but the authenticity of its origin will be debated for decades.

1941
The first 'Emergency' Liberty ship is launched in America and christened the SS *Patrick Henry*. He was the Revolutionary who proclaimed 'Give me liberty or give me death', although he himself owned more than 200 slaves. In all the US will build more than 2,000 Liberty cargo ships during the Second World War.

1960
Bank Underground Station in London switches on Europe's first 'moving pavement' or travelator.

28
SEPTEMBER

1066

William 'the Conqueror', the Duke of Normandy, lands at Pevensey to begin his conquest of England and become King William I. He is known, quite respectfully, as Le Bâtard (Bastard) de Normandy, illegitimacy being a badge of honour if your father is rich and powerful.

1995

With the signing of the Oslo 2 Accords, Palestinian self-government in the West Bank is agreed.

1996

Captured by the Taliban, Mohammad Najibullah, President of Afghanistan, is castrated then dragged behind a truck until he dies. His remains are hung from a traffic light.

2000

The Second Intifada, or Palestinian uprising, begins when Israeli politician Ariel Sharon, surrounded by hundreds of riot police, makes a provocative visit to the Temple Mount compound in Jerusalem, home of the Al-Aqsa Mosque, the third-holiest site of Islam. Palestinians believe he is asserting Israeli supremacy over the mosque.

2011

The German Quandt family confirm that patriarch Günther Quandt, founder of BMW cars, was a member of the Nazi Party who used over 50,000 slave-labourers.

29
SEPTEMBER

1902

French writer Émile Zola dies, possibly murdered by those opposed to his support of Alfred Dreyfus, the Jewish Army officer unjustly accused of treason. Zola dies from carbon monoxide poisoning from the fire in his bedroom, but the examining magistrate tests the room's fire and chimney on guinea pigs, which all survive unscathed.

1916

John D. Rockefeller becomes the world's first billionaire.

1962

The fourth country to launch a satellite (after the US, the USSR and the UK), Canada sends Alouette into orbit.

1972

After Japan finally apologizes for the atrocities perpetrated in the Rape of Nanking, Tokyo and Beijing re-establish diplomatic relationships.

1988

NASA launches the Discovery shuttle, its first manned mission since the Challenger disaster over two years ago.

2008

Following the bankruptcy of both Lehman Brothers and Washington Mutual, the Dow Jones Average drops 777.68, the greatest single-day loss in history.

30
SEPTEMBER

1630
John Billington becomes the first person to be executed in England's Plymouth colony in the New World when he is hanged for the murder of a fellow *Mayflower* passenger.

1888
Early in the morning Jack the Ripper strikes twice, killing Lizzie Stride and Katherine Eddowes.

1938
British Prime Minister Neville Chamberlain returns from signing the Munich Agreement (allowing Germany to seize part of Czechoslovakia) and a peace treaty with Germany. He announces 'peace for our time'.

1949
Mao Tse-Tung is elected leader of the new People's Republic of China, which comes into being the following day.

1955
American actor James Dean is killed in his Porsche Spyder sports car. A legend arises that the car is cursed and that its recycled parts will be used in other death cars.

1

OCTOBER

1800

Spain sells its claim to the Louisiana Territory to France. Far more than the modern state of that name, this represents the central third of the USA running from the Gulf of Texas up to the Canadian border.

1962

US troops and National Guardsmen are mobilized to deal with riots following the enrolment of African-American student James H. Meredith at the University of Mississippi. Television crews are attacked and their vans burned by racist mobs brandishing firearms and petrol bombs.

1964

The first Japanese bullet trains run between Tokyo and Osaka, routinely travelling at speeds of up to 200 mph (320 kph). In 1979 a maglev version will reach more than 321 mph (517 kph) on a test track.

1970

The state funeral of Egyptian President Abdel Nasser descends into chaos as scores of mourners are either trampled to death by the crowd or clubbed to death by the military trying to restore order.

2
OCTOBER

1871
Mormon leader Brigham Young is arrested for bigamy. All in all he will have fifty-five wives and fifty-six children.

1887
Violet Jessop is born. Becoming an ocean liner stewardess, she will survive three disasters: the collision of RMS *Olympic* in 1911; the sinking of the *Titanic* in 1912; and the mining of the *Britannic* in 1916.

1904
British author Graham Greene is born and will be recruited into MI6 by his sister, Elizabeth, so he can conduct missions under guise of travelling to research his books. His handler is Soviet double agent Kim Philby.

1935
Italy invades Abyssinia (Ethiopia) and, after a year of indiscriminate bombing and gassing, Emperor Haile Selassie will flee leaving the Italians in control.

1937
Dominican dictator Rafael Trujillo orders the slaughter of thousands of Haitians living in the borderlands of his country. Like Fidel Castro, Trujillo in his youth toyed with being a Hollywood extra, appearing in the closing scene of *Casablanca*.

3
OCTOBER

1226

The death of St Francis of Assisi, who in 1223 created the first Nativity scene, beginning a popular myth. The Magi actually arrived two years after the birth of Jesus.

1849

American writer Edgar Allan Poe is found 'in great distress' on the streets of Baltimore and will die four days later with speculation as to the cause of death ranging from rabies to poison. Always an oddball – he was nearly thirty when he married his thirteen-year-old cousin – Poe penned the first full-length detective novel, *The Murders in the Rue Morgue*.

1952

With the UK consuming a large part of the world's tea production, there is a national sigh of relief at the announcement that tea rationing will end.

1990

The end of the Second World War arrives at last with the reunification of East and West Germany. Until today there was no single, cohesive Germany to sign the formal peace treaty.

1995

Former American football star O. J. Simpson is found not guilty of stabbing his ex-wife Nicole and her friend, Ronald Goldman, to death.

4
OCTOBER

1535
Miles Coverdale's English translation of the Bible is printed, the first English edition of the complete work.

1669
The Dutch master painter Rembrandt dies in Amsterdam. In 1633 he inserted a 'd' into his name, signing as Rembrandt or even RemBrandt. This might be a reference to the dark tone of his work since 'rem' is the Dutch for obstructed or dimmed while 'brandt' means light.

1877
Historically secretive and insular, China opens its first Western embassy in London, with another opening on this same date in Washington DC next year.

1927
A former associate of the Ku Klux Klan who cut his teeth on a mountain memorial for the Confederate forces at Stone Mountain in Georgia, American sculptor Gutzon Borglum starts work on the presidential statues at Mount Rushmore.

1952
Dr Paul Zoll of the Harvard Medical School in America fits the first pacemaker to patient David Schwartz. Although worn externally, the device corrects Schwartz's cardiac arrhythmia, but it will be another six years before internal devices are available.

5

OCTOBER

1728

A celebrated spy of French King Louis XV is born. Madame d'Éon will connive against the Habsburgs and Russia, and will become famed and feared for her proficiency with a sword. When d'Éon dies in London in 1810, she turns out to be a he.

1892

Some of the last of the desperados of the Old West of the USA, five members of the Dalton Gang are gunned down in the streets of Coffeyville in Kansas by locals after they try to rob both the town's banks.

1930

On her maiden voyage to India, the British R-101 airship, then the world's largest aircraft, crashes in France killing forty-eight of the fifty-four on board. British Air-Minister Lord Thompson had brought along luggage equivalent to the weight of 30 extra passengers.

1936

With the intention of highlighting the plight of the unemployed in the depressed north-east of the UK, some 200 men set out on the 300-mile (480-km) Jarrow March from Jarrow to London where the Government refuses to grant audience to the group's leaders.

6
OCTOBER

1908

The Austro-Hungarian Empire takes one of the early steps towards the First World War by annexing Bosnia and Herzegovina from Turkey.

1927

Presented as the first feature-length 'talkie', the American movie *The Jazz Singer* is released. But, with the sound on separate long-play records and only about 350 words spoken throughout, should this qualify? This system has been used for years for shorter films and the first soundtrack-on-film systems are already being developed.

1973

With most of the country in prayer and deep reflection on the Jewish Day of Atonement, or Yom Kippur, Israel is attacked on two fronts by Egypt and Syria. Israel will win the war but will neither forgive not forget the Arabs for mounting a surprise attack on such a day.

1976

An Air Cuba flight from Barbados to Jamaica is brought down by two bombs shortly after take-off. All seventy-eight on board are killed, including the twenty-four members of the Cuban fencing team returning from winning gold at the Central American and Caribbean Championships. The finger will point to CIA-backed anti-Castro elements.

7
OCTOBER

1737

Massive waves being driven by a super cyclone smash into the Bay of Bengal to destroy thousands of small boats anchored there and kill perhaps 300,000 of those living on the crowded shorelines.

1985

The Italian cruise-ship *Achille Lauro* is seized by Palestinian terrorists off Egypt. The next day, they shoot 69-year-old disabled American Jew, Leon Klinghoffer, in his wheelchair, and throw him over the side. Palestine Liberation Organization spokesman Farouq Qaddumi will spitefully suggest Klinghoffer's terminally ill widow, Marilyn, had killed him for the insurance money but the PLO later admit responsibility.

2001

In response to the 9/11 attacks on New York and the Pentagon, the US launches Operation Enduring Freedom in Afghanistan, beginning by bombing airfields and bases in Kandahar and Kabul as well as al-Qaeda training camps in Jalalabad.

2006

Campaigning Russian journalist Anna Politkovskaya is shot dead in the lift of her block of flats in Moscow. It is still not known who ordered the killing, but most consider that her 2004 book, *Putin's Russia*, earned her powerful and ruthless enemies.

8
OCTOBER

1093

St Mark's Basilica in Venice is consecrated. Cafés in the square outside will be the scene of notoriety in 2013, when tourists from Rome are charged £85 for four liquor coffees.

1871

The Great Fire of Chicago breaks out with flames so tall that they span the Chicago River, only dying out when they reach Lake Michigan.

1905

German hairstylist Karl Nessler demonstrates in public the permanent wave. Having perfected his technique on Frau Nessler, who is absent with all her hair burnt off, he neglects to tell the enraptured audience that the results are achieved with an application of cow's urine.

1912

The Balkan League, comprising Greece, Montenegro, Serbia and Bulgaria, declares war on Turkey in the First Balkan War.

2005

The Kashmir earthquake kills over 100,000 and leaves over three million displaced and homeless.

9
OCTOBER

1874

The Mounties arrive at Fort Hamilton in the Cypress Hills, Saskatchewan, to bring law and order to Canada's western territories. An illegal whisky trading post, the fort is commonly known as Fort Whoop-Up.

1967

Che Guevara is executed. Ambushed in the Yuro Ravine in Bolivia, he was taken alive but subsequently riddled with bullets by his CIA/Bolivian captors to make it look as if he had died in the firefight.

1974

German businessman Oskar Schindler dies penniless. The extent of help he gave to Jews during the Second World War and his motives for doing so will continue to be hotly debated. But he will be declared a Righteous Gentile and be buried on Mount Zion in Israel, the only member of the Nazi Party to be thus honoured.

1991

The first Sumo wrestling tournament to be staged outside Japan takes place in London's Royal Albert Hall.

2008

Feeling the chilly wind of global recession, the Icelandic Government has to take control of the country's three major banks to prevent the nation's impending bankruptcy.

10
OCTOBER

1913

President Woodrow Wilson detonates an explosion by remote control from the White House to clear the last few yards of the Panama Canal.

1963

French diva Édith Gassion – Edith Piaf – dies of liver cancer at the age of forty-seven.

1967

The Outer Space Treaty comes into force. Originally signed only by Russia, America and the UK, it aims to prevent a country placing weapons systems on the Moon or anywhere else in space. By 2014 more than one hundred countries will have signed up.

1985

Hollywood giants Yul Brynner and Orson Welles die. Welles will have a pauper's funeral after arguments between ex-wives and offspring as to who was going to pay. In the end his widow, Paola Mori, who had thrown him out the previous year, will book a cheap room in a shabby district of Los Angeles, and only allow nine people to attend. She bans Welles's other former wives and most of his friends.

11
OCTOBER

1968

René Lévesque founds the Parti Québécois, a political party which aims to separate the province of Quebec from Canada as a sovereign state in its own right.

1972

Institutionalized racism in the US Navy is brought to global attention with the near-mutiny of 200 black sailors on USS *Kitty Hawk*, an aircraft carrier on active service off Vietnam. Nineteen of the rioters will later face charges.

1976

It is reported in the West that China's so-called Gang of Four, including Jiang Qing, the widow of Chairman Mao, have been arrested in Beijing for treason.

1979

Cuban President Fidel Castro is in New York to speak at the United Nations. On a visit to that city in 1995 he complains about potholes in the roads.

1987

Operation Deepscan, which has been looking for the Loch Ness Monster in Scotland, comes to an end. Using sophisticated scanning equipment, the project has cost £1 million, but declares the Loch free of prehistoric life. The monster was first mentioned in the sixth century.

12
OCTOBER

1810

To celebrate the marriage of Bavarian Crown Prince Ludwig to Princess Therese, the royal family holds a public festival in Munich, giving birth to the annual Oktoberfest.

1892

The Bellamy or Flag salute that is to be made during the Pledge of Allegiance to the Flag is demonstrated in the US. This calls for the right arm to be brought out from the chest at a raised angle of 45 degrees towards the flag with the palm down. Italian dictator Benito Mussolini will adopt a similar salute for his fascists, and after Adolf Hitler follows suit America will abandon the practice.

1915

During the First World War, British nurse Edith Cavell faces a German firing squad in Brussels after being found guilty of helping Allied soldiers escape. The Allies condemn the Germans while keeping quiet about their own executions of women.

1984

In the most audacious action by the Irish Republican Army ever, the Grand Hotel in Brighton, hosting the Conservative Party Conference, is bombed. Five people are killed as the bomb causes several floors to collapse, but Prime Minister Margaret Thatcher and her Cabinet, the intended targets, escape with their lives.

13
OCTOBER

54
Unpopular because of his ungainly appearance, the enlightened Roman Emperor Claudius dies. Possibly he is poisoned by his wife, Agrippina, to make way for her son, Nero.

1917
After three children claim to have encountered the Virgin Mary, a crowd of about 70,000 gather at Fátima in Portugal.

1930
There is silence in the German Reichstag today as 107 of Hitler's newly elected Nazis arrive to take their seats.

1988
The results of exhaustive radiocarbon dating tests on the Turin Shroud are announced: it dates from between 1260 and 1390, a time-span that matches the peak of traffic in Europe of faked religious artefacts and icons.

1997
The British-built ThrustSSC, a jet-powered car, breaks the sound barrier on the ground by travelling at 764 mph (1,229 kph) at Black Rock Desert in Nevada.

2010
After spending sixty-nine days trapped 700 feet (213 m) underground in the collapsed San José Gold and Copper Mine, the last of thirty-three Chilean miners is winched to safety.

14
OCTOBER

1066

William of Normandy (the Conqueror) wins the Battle of Hastings in England, which in fact takes place seven miles away from that town on Senlac Hill. The notion that the defeated King Harold is downed with an arrow in his eye will come from an unclear image on the Bayeux Tapestry (which is actually an embroidery).

1808

France annexes the province of Ragusa (Dubrovnik), which is nowadays in Croatia. The province has long specialized in building a type of massive ship, capable of carrying varied cargoes, which is called an argosy in English as a corruption of the name of the port.

1926

Winnie the Pooh is first published by English author A. A. Milne who takes the name from Winnipeg, affectionately known to all as Winnie, a popular bear donated to London Zoo by Canada.

1944

German Field Marshal Erwin Rommel dies, reportedly from injuries sustained months earlier when his staff car was strafed off the road by enemy fighters. In fact, he has been condemned for his part in the bomb-plot to kill Hitler but has been allowed to take poison and kill himself.

15
OCTOBER

1860

Eleven-year-old Grace Bedell of Westfield, New York, writes to future US President Abraham Lincoln to tell him he would look better with a beard. Previously clean-shaven, Lincoln takes this advice and, when visiting Westfield in February 1861, he makes a point of meeting Grace.

1946

Former head of the Gestapo, Hermann Göring takes poison in his cell to cheat the Nuremberg hangman. The enduring mystery as to how he got the poison will be solved in 2005 when Herbert Lee Stivers, a nineteen-year-old private in the US Army at the time, admits he smuggled it in at the behest of a local girl.

1964

Soviet leader Nikita Khrushchev is 'retired' as power in Moscow is assumed by Leonid Brezhnev and Alexei Kosygin.

1967

The ocean liner *Queen Mary* is decommissioned and will become a floating hotel at Long Beach in California.

1969

American cities are gridlocked today by the largest demonstration in its history as, in co-ordinated but peaceful rallies, more than two million protest against the continuation of the war in Vietnam.

16

OCTOBER

1384

Despite being a woman, Jadwiga is crowned 'King' of Poland. The title is given partly to show that she is ruler in her own right, not just a queen by marriage.

1814

The main tanks at the Meux Brewery in London's St Giles district rupture, sending 323,000 imperial gallons (1.5 million litres) of beer gushing through the streets. While many enjoy this unexpected bounty, at least eight people die, most drowning in their basement slums.

1834

The ancient Palace of Westminster, the home of the British Parliament, is destroyed by fire, to be replaced by the Victorian Gothic edifice that stands today.

1859

American abolitionist John Brown leads his ill-fated raid on the arsenal at Harper's Ferry in Virginia to steal guns for an armed slaves' rebellion. A young officer called Robert E. Lee is sent to capture the raiders, and Brown and most of his companions are hanged.

1996

Following the massacre of schoolchildren at Dunblane in Scotland, the British Government announces it will ban the possession of handguns.

17
OCTOBER

1931
Chicago gangster Al Capone is convicted of tax evasion and sentenced to eleven years.

1933
Having abandoned his native Germany because of Nazi death threats, physicist Albert Einstein arrives in America to take up a position at Princeton University. He will become an American citizen in 1940.

1943
The longest graveyard in the world, the Japanese Burma Railway between Bangkok in Thailand and Rangoon in Burma, is completed, with more than 100,000 Allied prisoners of war and Asian slaves dying in its construction. Countless bridges had to be built, including Bridge 227, the notorious Bridge over the River Kwai, or Buffalo River.

1973
Arab oil-states vote to increase the price of crude oil by a staggering 70 per cent. The following day they agree an oil embargo. This is their punishment for Western support of Israel in the Yom Kippur War.

1980
British Queen Elizabeth II makes the first royal visit to the Vatican since King Henry VIII broke from the Roman Catholic Church to form the Church of England in 1534.

18
OCTOBER

1356

The strongest earthquake in European history hits Basel in Switzerland with an estimated magnitude of 7.1 to completely flatten the town. All buildings in a 20-mile radius (32 km) – churches and castles included – are flattened.

1842

American inventor Samuel Morse carries out a successful test of underwater telegraph lines. Telegraph poles and lines will be colonized by climbing-plants, earning the network the nickname of the Grapevine, the source of all information and gossip.

1851

The first edition of American writer Herman Melville's *The Whale* is published. Later editions will carry the title *Moby Dick*. The name is possibly inspired by reports in the 1830s of a massive white whale attacking shipping off the Chilean island of Mocha, where the creature is known as Mocha Dick.

1922

The British Broadcasting Company (as the BBC is then called) is founded.

2007

A suicide-bomb attack on former Pakistani Prime Minister Benazir Bhutto's motorcade in Karachi kills 139 and injures over 500 but misses the intended target. She is assassinated two months later.

19

OCTOBER

1781

The British Army under General Cornwallis surrenders to the American Revolutionaries at Yorktown, prompting Britain to seek an end to the American Revolutionary War.

1812

Having arrived in Moscow to find it deserted and in flames in a 'scorched-earth' Russian retreat, Napoleon Bonaparte and his starving French Army begin their long march home. They will fall prey to snipers, pinprick attacks, starvation and, of course, the Russian winter. Of the 500,000 who marched into Russia perhaps only 20,000 will come out.

1921

Lisbon's 'Bloody Night', during which Portuguese Prime Minister António Granjo and other leading politicians are murdered in a coup.

1943

The antibiotic streptomycin is developed. It will become the first effective weapon against tuberculosis, which will become a rare condition until the advent of AIDS brings a resurgence of cases.

1970

British Petroleum announces the first oil-strike in the North Sea.

2003

Mother Teresa of Calcutta is beatified by Pope Paul II.

20
OCTOBER

1818

After the War of 1812, America and Britain finally decide on the 49th Parallel as the definitive border between the United States and Canada. By the year 2000, over 75 per cent of Canada's population will be living within a 100 miles (160 km) of this line.

1890

English explorer Sir Richard Burton dies in Trieste. He is best remembered for his translation of *The Arabian Nights (The Thousand and One Nights)* and for arranging the English publication of the *Kama Sutra*, which is not what most imagine. Sexual advice is restricted to just one of the thirty-six chapters of this Indian book, which is more of a lifestyle guide than anything else.

1935

The Chinese Communists' Long March, a desperate military retreat from the Nationalists, finishes today in Yan'an.

1941

After numerous Serbian partisan attacks, Field Marshal Wilhelm Keitel, head of the German occupying force, has ordered one hundred civilians shot for every German dead. Following another attack, the SS marches into Kragujevac, Serbia's fourth-largest city, and guns down an estimated 5,000 boys and men aged between ten and sixty.

21
OCTOBER

1805

British Admiral Horatio Nelson is shot during the Battle of Trafalgar and taken below to die. Although he was missing assorted bits and pieces, Nelson never wore an eye patch.

1858

Orpheus in the Underworld, an operetta by French composer Jacques Offenbach, opens in Paris to mixed reviews. The piece becomes doomed in the eyes of moralists when cancan girls seize on its 'Infernal Galop' as their signature tune.

1921

American President Warren G. Harding becomes the first occupant of the White House to speak out against the lynching of African Americans in the South.

1931

The Sakurakai, a secret cabal of Japanese officers, mounts an abortive coup to take over the country they believe to have become decadent and unpatriotic. They have tried before and will try again.

1944

During the Battle of Leyte Gulf in the Philippines, HMAS *Australia* becomes the first target of a Japanese kamikaze or suicide attack.

22
OCTOBER

1707

Poor navigation has British naval commander Sir Cloudesley Shovell believing his fleet to be off the coast of Brittany, whereas he is in fact heading for the rocks off the Scilly Isles. In one of the worst UK naval disasters of all time, four of the ships go down with over 1,400 lives lost.

1784

Russia cements its claim to Alaska by establishing a settlement on Kodiak Island.

1926

Born Erik Weisz, the Hungarian-American stage magician Harry Houdini receives the injuries that will kill him. J. Gordon Whitehead, visiting Houdini in his dressing room, asks if it is true he can withstand punches to the abdomen and, without giving Houdini the chance to tense his muscles, unleashes a flurry of blows causing the internal damage that will kill the star.

1934

Named Public Enemy Number One by J. Edgar Hoover (Director of the Federal Bureau of Investigation) after the death of John Dillinger, bank robber Pretty Boy Floyd is gunned down by police and the FBI in a cornfield in Ohio. Like his contemporary Baby-Face Nelson, Floyd hated his nickname and was prone to shoot at those who so addressed him.

23

OCTOBER

42BC

Just two years after his involvement in the assassination of his adoptive father Julius Caesar, Roman politician Brutus commits suicide after his army is routed at Philippi by the combined forces of Octavian, later the Emperor Augustus, and Mark Antony.

1642

The first full-scale battle in the English Civil War is pitched at Edgehill in the Cotswolds, resulting in a bloody draw. Proportionally, the war will have higher British casualties than the First World War, with over 250,000 dead out of a total population of about 6 million.

1739

The War of Jenkins' Ear begins between Britain and Spain. It is named after the Welsh Captain Robert Jenkins who appeared before parliament waving aloft his severed ear in a pickle-jar, asserting it had been cut off by a Spaniard who boarded his ship off Florida to accuse him of being a smuggler – which he was.

1935

On the orders of the Mafia, maverick mobster Dutch Schultz and his accountant Otto Berman are shot in the Palace Chophouse, Newark, New Jersey, and will die the following day. Berman is the one who coined 'It ain't personal; it's business.' Just weeks before his death, Schultz had buried $7 million in upstate New York. Treasure hunters are still looking for it.

24
OCTOBER

1537

Jane Seymour, the third wife of English King Henry VIII, dies today after giving birth to a son, the future King Edward VI.

1818

German composer Felix Mendelssohn gives his first concert in Berlin; he is nine years old.

1901

Desperate to raise funds, American adventurer Annie Edson Taylor is the first person to go over Niagara Falls in a barrel and survive. Today is her sixty-third birthday.

1929

The Wall Street Stock Market Crash begins in earnest triggering the Great Depression in the US.

1945

The United Nations Organization is formed at a ceremony in the American capital Washington DC. It will soon become known simply as the United Nations.

2003

Returning from New York to London, the supersonic aeroplane Concorde ends its last passenger flight.

25
OCTOBER

1415

The French nobility is culled in dramatic fashion at the Battle of Agincourt. English archers take out over 1,500 knights and over 5,000 men-at-arms.

1854

Through confusion in orders, the British Light Brigade charges the Russian Army during the Battle of Balaclava in the Crimean War.

1917

The Storming of the Winter Palace in St Petersburg, Russia: Lenin's Bolsheviks charge into this former residence of the Russian Tsar, currently the seat of the Provisional Government, to find it empty. The only fatalities are would-be revolutionaries shooting at each other in the dark.

1920

King Alexander of Greece dies of septicaemia caused by a monkey bite. On 2 October his German Shepherd dog had got into a fight with a palace ape, and the king was bitten when he tried to separate them.

1983

Less than a week after Cuban-backed militia execute Grenadan Prime Minister Maurice Bishop and thirteen of his ministers, American forces invade the island and take control.

26
OCTOBER

1881

The 'Gunfight at the OK Corral' actually takes place on a vacant lot in Tombstone, Arizona. The confrontation between the Clantons' outlaw gang and Marshal Virgil Earp, assisted by his brothers and others including Wyatt Earp's friend 'Doc' Holliday, lasts about thirty seconds and leaves three dead, all on the Clantons' side.

1979

The President of South Korea, Park Chung Hee, is 'accidentally shot' by his Head of Intelligence, Kim Jae Kyu who had been arguing with Hee's bodyguard, Cha Chi Chul, as to who was best to guard the premier. Fisticuffs turn to gunfire between the two factions with Hee and five others killed.

1985

The freehold title of Uluru, better known to white Australians and tourists as Ayres Rock, is returned to the Native Australian Anangu tribe in whose lands it stands.

2002

Three days after the Dubrovka Theatre in Moscow was taken over by Chechen Separatists who threatened to blow up the building along with the 850-strong audience, the siege comes to a calamitous conclusion. Russian Special Forces pump an unspecified gas into the building killing all the terrorists and about 130 hostages.

27
OCTOBER

1914

Welsh writer Dylan Thomas is born. His *Under Milk Wood*, read by Richard Burton and broadcast in 1954, will upset the moral dignity of the British Broadcasting Corporation. Only afterwards will the BBC realize that the location of the action, the fictitious Welsh village of Llareggub, is 'bugger all' backwards. British author Terry Pratchett will follow suit with his country of Llamedos in his *Discworld* series.

1936

The American socialite Wallis Simpson is granted a divorce from her second husband. This frees her for British King Edward VIII who will abdicate in order to marry her.

1962

US Air Force Major Rudolph Anderson, Jr. is the only casualty of the Cuban Missile Crisis when his spy-plane is shot down over the island.

1986

The deregulation of the London Money Market results in today's so-called 'Big Bang' with reverberations that cause disastrous echoes into the next millennium.

2003

Suicide bombers target the Red Cross compound and police stations in Baghdad, killing thirty-five and injuring more than 200.

28

OCTOBER

1492

Christopher Columbus lands in Cuba. Despite all the places named after him on mainland America, he never actually sets foot there; he only visits the offshore islands, never imagining for a minute what lay over the horizon.

1636

The first university in America is founded today at Cambridge, Massachusetts with a legacy from Puritan minister John Harvard. The seated statue of the benefactor in Harvard's courtyard is actually modelled on a nameless student.

1962

The Cuban Missile Crisis comes to a close with Soviet leader Nikita Khrushchev announcing the withdrawal of all Soviet nuclear missiles from the island. In return, the US promises never to invade Cuba. American Secretary of State Dean Rusk has summed up the situation by saying: 'I think the other fellow just blinked'.

1971

The British House of Commons votes by a majority of 112 to join the European Common Market.

1979

Chairman Hua Kuo-Feng, the first Chinese leader to visit the UK, is greeted at Heathrow Airport by Prime Minister Margaret Thatcher.

29

OCTOBER

1618

Having fallen out of favour with English Queen Elizabeth I, the adventurer Sir Walter Raleigh is executed in London.

1922

Having arranged for a mass fascist March on Rome, Benito Mussolini is invited by King Victor Emanuel to form a government. In actual fact only a few hundred of his followers form the protest group, and he himself travels by first-class train from Milan to Rome, rushing to mount a white stallion and lead the parade for the sake of the press.

1975

With dictator General Franco close to death it is announced that the monarchy will return to Spain after a gap of forty-four years as his designated heir Prince Juan Carlos is ready to take over.

1998

Thirty-six years after he became the first American to orbit the earth, the seventy-seven-year-old Senator John Glenn becomes the oldest person to go into space when he re-joins the NASA programme to take off in Discovery STS-95.

2012

Hurricane Sandy comes out of the Caribbean to hit the American east coast, killing 160. The official naming of storms began in 1945.

30

OCTOBER

1485

The Yeomen of the Guard is formed by British King Henry VII on the day of his coronation. A bodyguard of the monarch, the Guard is the oldest British military corps.

1925

London office worker William Taynton becomes the first face ever to appear on television after he is grabbed by Scottish inventor John Logie Baird for the experiment.

1984

The latest in a long line of clergy to be murdered by the Polish Government, the body of Father Jerzy Popieluszko, an outspoken supporter of Lech Walesa and Solidarity, is found in the Wloclawek Reservoir. After an unsuccessful attempt to run him over in the street, the Polish Secret Police have simply kidnapped him and battered him to death.

1988

At the Olympic Stadium in Seoul, South Korea, 6,516 identically dressed couples are married by their Moonie leader, Sun Myung Moon, who has matched the couples at random.

1991

American President George Bush opens the Middle East Peace Conference in Madrid, arranged by the US and the Soviet Union. It is the first time for forty-three years that Israel has had peace talks with all its Arab neighbours.

31
OCTOBER

1517

German priest Martin Luther supposedly nails his Ninety-Five Theses to the door of All Saints' Church in Wittenberg, helping initiate the Reformation. Luther was violently anti-Semitic, and in the kind of chilling echo that history is good at, a German politician involved in setting the Holocaust in train will also be called Martin Luther.

1940

The Battle of Britain ends. The Germans have lost four times the aircrew lost by the Allies. Despite its iconic status, the Spitfire has played a lesser role than the more stable Hurricane.

1961

The embalmed body of Stalin is removed from Lenin's tomb as part of the programme to reduce his standing in Soviet history. He is re-buried outside the Kremlin.

1984

The Prime Minister of India, Mrs Indira Gandhi, is shot dead in the garden of her New Delhi home by two of her Sikh bodyguards. She has ignored warnings against employing Sikhs after she ordered the invasion and desecration of the Sikh temple at Amritsar a few months ago.

2011

The United Nations announces that the global population stands at seven billion.

1
NOVEMBER

1512

The ceiling of the Sistine Chapel is revealed to the public. It is a myth that Michelangelo painted it lying on his back atop towering scaffolding and that the ceiling is his work alone. In 1565, Daniele da Volterra will add several fig leaves to naked figures and repaint the naked St Catherine and St Blaise who, from some perspectives, originally appear to be locked in sexual intercourse.

1800

John Adams becomes the first US president to live in the White House when he moves in with his family.

1939

The first rabbit born of pioneering artificial insemination techniques is exhibited in New York.

1950

Two Puerto Rican Nationalists attack US President Harry Truman who is staying in the White House's guest quarters while the main building is being renovated. One of his guards is killed and two others wounded before the would-be assassins are subdued.

1988

In response to readers' demands, Jason Todd, the second Robin, is killed off in the story arc beginning in this month's edition of the *Batman* comic. He is dynamited off the pages by the Joker.

2
NOVEMBER

1755

The Austrian Archduchess Marie Antoinette is born. As French queen, she probably never uttered the infamous 'Let them eat cake' statement about peasants who could not afford bread. After the French Revolution of 1789 she will die on the guillotine.

1898

University of Minnesota student Johnny Campbell becomes the first cheerleader as he struts the touchline, leading the crowd in supportive chants for his American football team. Cheerleaders are male until 1923 and only during the Second World War, with the shortage of men, does cheerleading start to resemble what it is today.

1917

Britain issues the Balfour Declaration which indicates support for the foundation of a Jewish State in Palestine.

1930

Haile Selassie is crowned King of Kings of Ethiopia.

1947

The huge flying boat built by American tycoon Howard Hughes has its short maiden flight, never to fly again. The Hercules H-4 is nicknamed the Spruce Goose although it is made mainly of birch and is allegedly known informally as the Birch Bitch.

3

1783

Highwayman John Austin is the last man to be hanged on London's Tyburn Gibbet, which stands at modern Marble Arch.

1843

The statue of Nelson is winched into place on Nelson's Column, Trafalgar Square, London. The monument will become so iconic that during the Second World War Hitler, anticipating a successful invasion of Britain, plans to dismantle it and re-erect it in Berlin.

1941

Joseph Grew, the American ambassador in Tokyo, sends a coded cable to Washington, repeating his warnings that Japan is gearing up for a pre-emptive strike on the United States. Again his warnings are ignored. Pearl Harbor is attacked next month.

1957

The USSR launches Laika the dog into space orbit aboard Sputnik 2. There will be huge protests when it turns out she was poisoned by remote control before re-entry into earth's atmosphere.

1979

Wrongly believed by some to have become a spent force, the American Ku Klux Klan shoots dead five marchers on a Communist Party rally as it progresses through Greensboro in North Carolina.

4

NOVEMBER

1921

Japanese Prime Minister Hara Takashi is stabbed to death at Tokyo Station by right-wing rail-worker Nakaoka Kon'ichi who, to the surprise of many, will only serve thirteen years for a crime normally attracting the death sentence.

1956

Soviet tanks roll into Hungary to crush the rebellion that started last month.

1960

At the Gombe Stream National Park in Tanzania, Dr Jane Goodall films chimpanzees making and using crude tools.

1979

With the deposed Shah of Iran in America, a mob of Iranian students seizes the American Embassy in Tehran and takes fifty-two hostages, demanding the return of the Shah to Iran to face trial and execution for atrocities during his reign. The hostage crisis will last 444 days.

1980

Sixty-nine-year-old Ronald Reagan beats Jimmy Carter in the US elections, making him the oldest elected president of America.

2008

Barack Obama is elected the first African-American president of the US.

5

NOVEMBER

1605

The Catholic Gunpowder Plot, organized by Robert Catesby, is uncovered in the cellars under the House of Lords in London, where Guy Fawkes has stashed thirty-six barrels of gunpowder, ready to blow up the Protestant parliament sitting above. The conspirators are swiftly rounded up and executed.

1688

William of Orange lands with his Dutch fleet at Brixham on the south coast of England and marches on London to take the throne as William III. According to legend, orange carrots are bred from the purple originals to honour the House of Orange.

1925

The inspiration for James Bond, Sidney Reilly, aka Ace of Spies, is killed by the Soviet Secret Police somewhere outside Moscow. Working for the British Secret Service, the order for his death has come straight from Stalin.

1937

Adolf Hitler holds the first secret Lebensraum Meeting to decide how Germany can expand to get more living-space. Basically this boils down to deciding which countries to invade and in which order.

1943

American bombers accidentally hit the Vatican, causing extensive damage.

6
NOVEMBER

1810

Only in Australia would one find a Rum Hospital. Lachlan Macquarie, Governor of New South Wales, gives the valuable rum monopoly to a consortium of local businessmen on condition that part of their profits are used to build the Sydney Rum Hospital, parts of which still stand today.

1919

Hollywood silent-screen heart-throb Rudolph Valentino marries the actress Jean Acker, who has been involved in a lesbian love triangle. She changes her mind that night and locks him out of the bedroom. It is thought the marriage is never consummated.

1923

There are riots in Germany over hyperinflation. The German mark has sunk to 4,210,500,000,000 to the American dollar making bank-robbery and mugging crimes of the past: money is just not worth stealing any more. A loaf of bread costs 200 million marks and workers taking their wages home in wheelbarrows is a common sight.

1941

Giving a speech in Moscow, Soviet leader Joseph Stalin claims that the Soviet Union is nearing victory over the German invaders, of whom 4.5 million have, he said, been killed by the victorious Soviet forces. In reality the German forces will advance further into the USSR before the Soviets turn the tide.

7
NOVEMBER

1872

The *Mary Celeste* – not *Marie Celeste* – sails out of New York and into maritime lore. She will later be found abandoned but tales of the table being set for a meal and still-warm cups of tea are the stuff of fantasy. The ship's sextant and chronometer are missing, as is the only lifeboat, so apparently something caused the crew to abandon ship.

1960

Missiles and their launchers appear for the first time in the USSR's annual Red Square Parade as a clear message to the West.

1962

Eleanor Roosevelt dies. Despite her dislike of heterosexual intimacy, she married her father's cousin, Franklin D. Roosevelt, in 1905 but many think that the real love of her life was journalist Lorena Hickok whom she met while Hickok was covering FDR's presidential campaign. Just to complicate matters further, FDR had been conducting an affair with Lucy Mercer, his wife's social secretary.

1990

The last Soviet military parade takes place at Red Square, Moscow. The parades commemorate the Bolshevik revolution and victory over Nazi Germany.

8

1519

Spanish Conquistador Hernán Cortés arrives in Tenochtitlan to be met by Aztec Emperor Moctezuma, popularly rendered Montezuma. Legend says the Aztecs regarded the white-skinned people as gods but this is untrue, as is the story that Cortés will subdue Mexico with only a handful of men.

1895

While experimenting with electricity, German physicist Wilhelm Röntgen accidentally discovers rays that he does not fully understand, so he calls them X-rays, from the mathematical use of x for an unknown quantity.

1923

Adolf Hitler leads the abortive Beer Hall Putsch in an attempt to seize power in Bavaria and then Germany. He is charged with treason and given a five-year prison sentence, but will be released after nine months. He spends that time dictating *Mein Kampf* to cellmate Rudolf Hess.

1950

US Air Force Lieutenant Russell J. Brown, piloting an F-80 Shooting Star, takes out two North Korean M&G-15s in the first-ever jet-on-jet dogfight. The M&G is incorrectly known in the West as a Mig since the makers are Mikoyan and Gurevich and 'i' is the Russian for 'and'.

9
NOVEMBER

1799

Although he never quite learns to spell the French language properly, thirty-year-old Corsican Napoleon Bonaparte is appointed First Consul and Head of State of France. The last element of his name is correctly pronounced to sound like 'party'.

1938

Jews in major German and Austrian cities endure the Kristallnacht, the Night of Broken Glass, during which 1,000 synagogues are burnt and 7,000 shops and businesses looted by Nazi thugs.

1960

The first non-family member to head the corporation, Robert McNamara is appointed president of the Ford Motor Company; within weeks he will resign to join the newly formed Kennedy Administration as Secretary of State for Defense.

1963

In one of the worst mining disasters on record, the Mitsui Miike Coal Mine in Kyushu, Japan, is shattered by an underground explosion that kills nearly 500 and puts another 900 in hospital.

1965

Roger LaPorte, a twenty-two-year-old American pacifist, sets himself on fire outside the United Nations building in New York to protest about the war in Vietnam. Shocked witnesses try to douse the flames but he will die in hospital tomorrow.

10
NOVEMBER

1847

Dr James Simpson of Edinburgh delivers a talk to the Medico-Chirurgical Society of Edinburgh reporting the successful use of his newly developed chloroform in childbirth. Some religious leaders object since the Bible says that women are condemned to bring forth life through pain. But in 1853 Queen Victoria demands chloroform for her delivery of Prince Leopold, inspiring its widespread use.

1871

Welsh-born journalist Henry Morton Stanley finds his quarry, the Scottish missionary and explorer David Livingstone, in present-day Tanzania, but does not say 'Dr Livingstone, I presume?' The statement is invented the following year by the editor of the newspaper who had sent Stanley to Africa.

1960

After a six-day obscenity trial the previous month, Penguin Books is allowed to publish *Lady Chatterley's Lover* in the UK. The 200,000 print run sells out before lunch.

1965

The Northeast blackout, the biggest power-cut in history, is over as Ontario in Canada, New York and other US states are brought back on line. Popular myth will tell of a spike in the birth-rate nine months later but the figures actually show a drop.

11
NOVEMBER

1634

After a campaign by Bishop John Atherton of the Church of Ireland, the Irish House of Commons passes anti-homosexuality legislation. Atherton will fall foul of his own laws when he is caught in bed with his servant John Childe. Both men are hanged in December 1640.

1880

Australian bushranger Ned Kelly goes to the gallows outside Melbourne Gaol. When informed of the time of execution, he says: 'Such is life'.

1926

The United States institutes the system of numbering highways to create, among others, Route 66. Unfortunately for lovers of the song, the route no longer exists in its original form.

1938

Mary Mallon, the original Typhoid Mary, dies of pneumonia. A medical rarity, she was a typhoid-carrier who insisted on continuing to work, under pseudonyms, as a cook in New York. Responsible for countless deaths, she was eventually quarantined.

2000

The Kaprun funicular fire in Austria kills 155 skiers, many of them children. Their train is in an uphill tunnel when the fire breaks out and flames are rapidly fanned by the passage of air around the moving cars.

12

1035

King Canute of England, Denmark and Norway dies. He did indeed take his throne to the edge of the sea to show sycophantic courtiers that all power has its limitations and not even he could command the waves to be still.

1858

The original 'Daring young man on the flying trapeze', Frenchman Jules Léotard launches his new trapeze in a Paris circus. His self-designed costume bears his name to this day.

1954

Ellis Island closes its doors after processing more than fifteen million people into the US. Illiterate Jews admitted in the early 1900s refused to sign with a cross as this was associated with Christianity, so they made a circle, or 'kikel' as it is in Yiddish. Educated Jews coined 'kike' as an insult meaning circle-writer.

1978

The newly appointed Pope John Paul II takes his seat in the Basilica of St John Lateran as Bishop of Rome. Although St Peter's grabs all the limelight on papal occasions, it is the comparatively unimpressive St John's that is the mother church of the Catholic world.

2011

Besieged by accusations of corruption and scandal, Italian Prime Minister Silvio Berlusconi resigns.

1914

Co-founder of the Black Sun Press, which numbered Laurence Sterne and Ernest Hemingway among its writers, the fast-living Caresse Crosby is granted a patent for the first backless bra. Distracted by hedonistic adventures, she will sell the patent for $1,500 to a company that goes on to make a fortune.

1970

General Hafez al-Assad mounts a military coup and takes control of Syria.

1971

Mariner 9 goes into orbit around Mars but the planet is obscured by a dust-storm of incredible magnitude.

1974

Ronald deFeo, Jr. murders his mother, father and four siblings in their home in Amityville, New York. Next year the Lutz family will move in and start the *Amityville Horror* bandwagon with tall tales of cloven hoofprints in the snow outside and green slime oozing out of the walls inside.

1974

Activist Karen Silkwood is killed when her car is possibly run off the road outside Oklahoma City. A worker in the Kerr-McGee Fuel plant making plutonium pellets for nuclear reactors, she has already testified about safety concerns and the investigative papers she was known to be carrying are missing from her car.

14
NOVEMBER

1687

English actress Nell Gwyn dies of syphilis aged thirty-seven. Between 1663 and 1667 she dressed as a man, complete with stick-on beard, and went by the name of William Nell, but, dressed as a woman, she caught the roving eye of King Charles II when she met him at a theatre.

1889

New York World reporter Nellie Bly sets sail from New York today to put Jules Verne's 1873 novel *Around the World in Eighty Days* to the test. Making use of transport ranging from camels to Chinese junks, she will complete the trip in a record seventy-two days, six hours, eleven minutes and fourteen seconds.

1940

The German fire-bombing of Coventry in England leaves nearly two-thirds of the city either razed or seriously damaged. After the War a false story goes around that Prime Minister Winston Churchill knew of the attack in advance but did not put up additional air-defences in case the Germans realized that Bletchley Park had cracked the Enigma Code.

1991

In the second such incident this year alone, sacked US Postal Service worker Thomas McIlvaine marches back into the Royal Oak Sorting Office in Michigan and shoots at ex-colleagues. Four will die. The number of post office work-place shootings gives rise to 'going postal' as descriptive of uncontrollable rage.

15
NOVEMBER

1763

Charles Mason and Jeremiah Dixon start surveying the Mason-Dixon Line, which, in popular usage, will come to symbolize the North-South divide in America. Oddly enough, Dixie as a term for the South is unrelated, possibly deriving instead from early Louisiana banks' ten-dollar bills having the French ten, 'Dix' on the reverse.

1837

Isaac Pitman, a twenty-four-year-old teacher from Wiltshire in England, publishes his speedwriting system for business. In the US his brother Benjamin will make Pitman Shorthand famous by using it while sitting as the Court Recorder at the trials of those accused of complicity with John Wilkes Booth in the assassination of President Lincoln.

1899

The young Winston Churchill is captured by the Boers during the Boer War but will escape the stockade and make it home. In a twist of fate, the man who had taken him prisoner is Louis Botha. As the first prime minister of South Africa, he and Churchill will meet again in less combative surroundings.

1998

With bombers already en route to Baghdad to end Iraq's defiance of the UN, Saddam Hussein backs down and says he will allow UN weapons inspectors into the country.

16
NOVEMBER

1724

English thief Jack Sheppard is hanged at Tyburn. Non-violent and having escaped from jail four times, the public loved him. Over 200,000 turn out to wish him bon voyage. John Gay will make him into Macheath in the *Beggar's Opera*.

1848

Polish composer Frédéric Chopin gives his last public performance in London's Guildhall. Almost at death's door, he weighs less than ninety-nine pounds (45 kilos). He will die within a year, probably from tuberculosis.

1885

Canadian Louis Riel is hanged by the British for his leadership of the Red River and North-West Rebellions. This will be the last armed resistance to British rule in Canada.

1900

As Kaiser Wilhelm II of Germany tours Breslau in an open coach, Selma Schnapke, a circus performer-turned-shopkeeper, throws an axe at him, Apache-style, with considerable accuracy and efficiency. It narrowly misses the Kaiser's head and embeds itself into the interior of the carriage. She is later ruled to be insane.

1989

The first cracks in South African apartheid appear with the announcement that the country's beaches will no longer be segregated.

17
NOVEMBER

1558

England loses its first queen who ruled in her own right, Mary Tudor. Later remembered only as a drink, 'Bloody Mary' was an unkind epithet for her in that she only executed about 300 during her five-year reign, which, for a monarch of this era embarked on religious reform, showed considerable restraint. Her father, Henry VIII, killed a great many more people but is remembered more fondly.

1796

Catherine the Great of Russia expires but not, as popular myth relates, while riding a horse. As did Elvis, Evelyn Waugh, King George II of Great Britain and Lenny Bruce, she died on the toilet.

1959

The first duty-free shops in Britain open in Prestwick and Renfrew Airports with Heathrow being granted similar concessions early next year.

1997

Egyptian extremists, trying to weaken the government by destroying its revenue from the tourist trade, shoot tourists at the temple site of Deir el-Bahri at Luxor, killing sixty-two and injuring another twenty-six. Just weeks ago, a German tour-bus was strafed in Cairo resulting in nine dead.

18
NOVEMBER

1686

The pioneering French surgeon, Charles Felix de Tassy, performs the first successful surgery for an anal fistula on the person of King Louis XIV. He has killed three peasants perfecting the technique before attempting it on the royal behind.

1906

Alec Issigonis is born in Turkey. He will migrate to the UK in 1923 and in 1959 will design the Mini, which will become one of the bestselling cars of all time.

1977

Preparations begin for President Sadat's visit tomorrow as he becomes the first leader of an Arab state to visit Israel.

1978

Having moved his People's Temple congregation from California to Jonestown in Guyana, Jim Jones is pursued by Californian Congressman Leo Ryan, who is gunned down along with four others of his investigative party. Realizing he has gone too far, Jones orders the 910 cult members to commit suicide by cyanide. This is the largest cult-atrocity of modern times.

1984

British socialite and romantic novelist Dame Barbara Cartland is awarded the Bishop Wright Air Industry Award for devising the long-distance glider-tow used in the Second World War to take commandos deep into enemy territory.

19
NOVEMBER

1703

The original Man in the Iron Mask dies and is buried under the name of Marchioly. Kept in relative luxury in a succession of French prisons, he in fact wears a mask of black velvet with his captors told to treat him with respect but to kill him the moment he tries to talk of his identity.

1863

American President Abraham Lincoln delivers the Gettysburg Address, considered one of the nation's greatest speeches.

1984

In one of the most lethal industrial incidents in history, four massive tanks of liquid petroleum gas explode at the San Juanico storage depot outside Mexico City, killing about 600 people on the spot. The plumes of burning fuel shower the nearby barrio leaving more than 7,000 with horrendous burns and impact injuries.

1988

The troubled life of Greek shipping heiress Christina Onassis comes to a close with a heart attack in Argentina. After losing all her immediate family within a short space of time in the 1970s, she became addicted to prescription drugs and is four-times divorced at the time of her death, aged thirty-seven.

20
NOVEMBER

1820

The American whaling ship *Essex*, having been repeatedly rammed by a massive sperm whale, sinks in the South Pacific. Some of the crew survive ninety days in an open boat by eating one of the dead. The incident helps inspire Herman Melville's novel *Moby Dick*.

1910

The first time that planes are used in conflict, the Mexican Revolution begins under Francisco I. Madero.

1945

The Nuremberg Trials begin, prosecuting leading Nazi war criminals. At this point there is nothing in international law that covers genocide, which will not be illegal until the UN General Assembly ruling of 12 January 1951.

1947

The British Princess Elizabeth marries the Duke of Edinburgh, Philip Mountbatten, in Westminster Abbey in London.

1992

Fire sweeps through Windsor Castle in England, devastating over a hundred rooms and destroying countless works of art.

1995

British Princess Diana admits to having committed adultery on national television during her interview with Martin Bashir.

21
NOVEMBER

1783

French balloonists Jean François de Rozier and the Marquis d'Arlandes make the first untethered, manned hot-air balloon flight from the Bois de Boulogne, north of Paris, to land twenty-five minutes later in Butte-aux-Cailles, about 6 miles (9 km) away.

1910

The death of Russian author Leo Tolstoy. On the eve of his wedding to Sophia Andreyevna Behrs he presented his bride-to-be with written details of all the previous sexual encounters he had enjoyed and a note about his illegitimate child. The marriage is not a happy one.

1979

Ayatollah Khomeini of Iran orchestrates an attack on the American Embassy in Islamabad, Pakistan, by falsely accusing America of being involved in the current occupation of the Great Mosque in Mecca. In actual fact it is Muslim fundamentalists who have taken over the Mosque.

1990

The personification of Wall Street malpractice and perhaps the inspiration for movie character Gordon 'Greed-is-good' Gekko, Michael Milken, the so-called Junk Bond King, is jailed for ten years for financial impropriety and forced to hand over $600 million in fines and restitution. He will only serve twenty-two months.

22
NOVEMBER

1718

Operating out of secret moorings in the Carolinas, Edward Teach, aka the pirate Blackbeard, is killed in hand-to-hand combat with Lieutenant Robert Maynard of the British Royal Navy.

1774

British officer Robert Clive, aka Clive of India, dies of a drugs overdose at the age of forty-nine. As are many of his contemporaries, Clive is an opium addict; not until the 1920s will over-the-counter sales of the drug be banned in the UK and the USA.

1963

This is the bright and sunny day in Dallas, Texas, which will bring a close to the American Camelot with the assassination of US President John F. Kennedy. The conspiracy theories will start within a matter of days.

1997

Singer of rock band INXS, Michael Hutchence is found hanging from the door-fixtures of his hotel bedroom in Sydney, Australia. The death is ruled suicide but his girlfriend, Paula Yates, insists he would have been indulging in autoerotic asphyxia and got the timing wrong. Yates will die within a few years from a drugs overdose, as will her daughter, Peaches Geldof, in 2014.

23

NOVEMBER

1499

Having twice tried to raise armies and march on London, Perkin Warbeck, pretender to the English throne, is executed. He claimed to be the youngest son of King Edward IV, one of the Princes in the Tower who had escaped his would-be murderers.

1910

American homeopath Dr Crippen is hanged for the murder of his wife. Accused of dismembering her body and hiding the remains under the basement of their home in London, Crippen always maintained his wife, Cora, had disappeared back to the United States. Much later on, DNA tests will reveal the tissue samples to be male, although the tests will be hotly disputed.

2002

Organizers of the Miss World competition abandon plans to hold the event in Abuja, Nigeria, after Muslim protestors riot leaving more than a hundred dead on the streets of Kaduna.

2006

Having ended up on the wrong side of the Russian authorities, fugitive Russian secret agent Alexander Litvinenko dies in London after drinking tea that was laced with radioactive polonium-210. It is thought that he has been poisoned by Russian agent Andrei Lugovoi, but British demands for Lugovoi's extradition to stand trial are ignored by Moscow.

24

1434
The first recorded instance of the River Thames in London freezing. Throughout the so-called Little Ice Age of about 1350 to 1850 this will be a common occurrence, as will the Frost Fairs held on the frozen river.

1642
The Dutch navigator Abel Tasman sights a new island south of Australia that he names Van Diemen's Land after his ship's captain. Only later will it be renamed Tasmania.

1963
The first ever televised murder is broadcast internationally as nightclub owner Jack Ruby, a man with possible links to the Mob and the CIA, shoots Lee Harvey Oswald in the underground car park of Dallas Police Headquarters. Oswald, assassin of President John F. Kennedy, is being escorted very carelessly through the complex.

1991
Freddie Mercury of rock band Queen dies to become the UK's highest-profile victim of AIDS. Only yesterday did he issue a press release acknowledging he had the disease.

1998
The Queen's Speech today reveals the British Government's plans to ban the 700 hereditary peers from sitting or voting in the House of Lords.

25
NOVEMBER

1783

Three months after signing the Treaty of Paris to bring to a close the American War of Independence, the last British troops march out of New York.

1947

The Hollywood blacklist begins as the first batch of ten screenwriters and directors are fired after refusing to testify to the House Committee on Un-American Activities. They are all suspected of membership of the Communist Party.

1969

British pop star John Lennon returns his MBE medal in protest at Britain's continuing support of the American war in Vietnam.

1971

America's first successful skyjacker parachutes from the Portland-Seattle flight he has taken hostage. Known only under his alias, Dan or D.B. Cooper, he boarded the plane with a bomb, demanding parachutes and $200,000. His demands are met and Cooper bails out, the only undetected US air pirate.

1973

The Greek Army ousts the unpopular, brutal and self-appointed President Georgios Papadopoulos who came to power six years ago through another military coup.

26
NOVEMBER

1836

Nicknamed the Colossus of Roads, Scottish engineer John McAdam dies, his road-building techniques having revolutionized roads across Europe and America. His work only related to the robust substructure of the roads, not the dressing, and 'tarmac' is actually introduced much later.

1867

Having been placed on the electoral roll by mistake, Manchester shopkeeper Lily Maxwell becomes the first woman in the UK to cast a vote. Her vote will later be declared illegal.

1906

US President Teddy Roosevelt returns after his tour of Central America. This makes him the first serving president to travel beyond the confines of the United States.

1966

The world's first tidal-powered electricity-generating plant is opened by French President General de Gaulle on the Rance Estuary near St Malo. The power station had been designed as far back as 1955 by engineer Albert Caquot, but he was for years dismissed as an 'eco-nut'.

1983

The UK's biggest robbery is carried out with military precision as a small gang take £26 million's worth of gold bullion from the Brink's-MAT 'secure' warehouse at Heathrow Airport.

27
NOVEMBER

1835

Executed before a huge crowd at Newgate in London, James Pratt and John Smith become the last two men to be hanged for sodomy in the UK; in future those found guilty will be either jailed or transported to Australia.

1868

Lieutenant Colonel George Armstrong Custer of the US Cavalry leads an attack on a Cheyenne Native-American camp on the Washita River, killing women and children as well as warriors, and taking other non-combatants as hostages. Among these is seventeen-year-old Monahsetah, with whom Custer allegedly has two children. According to Native-American legend she will put an arrow through his body after he is killed at the Battle of the Little Big Horn in 1876.

1967

For the second time, French President General de Gaulle announces that he will block Britain's entry to the Common Market with a flat 'Non!'

1970

Pope Paul VI's visit to the Philippines does not get off to a good start. Screaming 'Death to superstition', a Bolivian surrealist painter called Benjamin Mendoza y Amor lunges at the pope with a knife, stabbing him in the chest as he walks through Manila Airport.

28
NOVEMBER

1859

The American writer Washington Irving dies. He was probably responsible for the myth that many Spaniards opposed Christopher Columbus's 1492 voyage to the East Indies (during which he landed in the Americas) because they feared he would sail off the edge of a flat earth.

1919

The American-born Nancy Astor, having been elected to the House of Commons, sits as Britain's first female MP. Later branded the Member for Berlin, as Lady Astor she will host gatherings of the pro-Nazi 'Cliveden Set' at her country house.

1950

The Battle of the Ch'ongch'on River in North Korea nears its mid-point. Failing to take seriously the threats from Chinese Foreign Minister Zhou Enlai that he would not sit by if American troops set foot in North Korea, their incursion across the border from South Korea has brought 300,000 Chinese troops across the Yalu River and into the Korean War.

1963

US President Lyndon B. Johnson announces that Cape Canaveral in Florida will be renamed Cape Kennedy.

1989

Romanian gymnast Nadia Comaneci defects by escaping to Hungary. She will eventually make her way to America.

800

Charlemagne, King of the Franks and King of Italy, arrives in Rome in support of Pope Leo III, who is facing a rebellion within the Church, including charges of adultery. The pope will reward Charlemagne by crowning him Holy Roman Emperor.

1777

The first civilian Spanish settlement is established in northern California and named San Jose.

1781

Having set out from Accra in Ghana with 442 African slaves on board, the crew of the slave ship *Zong* decide to lighten the load in a storm by throwing 168 men, women and children overboard. The ship is owned by a consortium based in Liverpool, England, who have taken out insurance on the 'cargo'. The only litigation in the UK will centre on whether the insurance company should pay for the loss of the slaves.

1814

The Times of London becomes the first newspaper to be printed on a steam-powered press.

1830

The November Insurrection, the armed rebellion of Poland against Russian rule, begins. Numerically inferior, the rebel armies are crushed by October 1831, with Moscow pronouncing that Poland is henceforth an integral part of Russia.

30
NOVEMBER

1835

Samuel Langhorne Clemens is born. Working in his youth as a Mississippi riverboat pilot he will take his pen-name from the call of the man with the easy job of taking depth-soundings with a lead-weighted line (hence 'swinging the lead'). This line has three markings with the middle one, or the Mark Twain, indicating two-fathoms and safe passage ahead.

1900

Irish playwright and poet Oscar Wilde dies penniless of cerebral meningitis, possibly syphilitic, in a squalid Parisian boarding house. In 1909 he will be re-buried in the Père-Lachaise Cemetery.

1934

The British train *Flying Scotsman* becomes the first steam-locomotive to be authenticated as having tipped the hundred miles per hour mark.

1939

The Soviet Union invades Finland, beginning the Winter War. Finnish troops run out of anti-tank guns so they use improvised weapons including bottles partly filled with petrol or other incendiary material. They name these Molotov Cocktails after Soviet Foreign Minister Vyacheslav Molotov. The Finns also field the greatest sniper in history, Simo Häyhä, known to the Russians as the White Death. Using open sights to prevent sun-glint on telescopics betraying his position, Häyhä also fills his mouth with snow so his breath cannot be seen.

1

DECEMBER

1913

Henry Ford institutes the conveyor-belt assembly line, which can turn out a Model T car in just over ninety minutes. Although hailed the first such system, sixteenth-century Venetian boatyards could turn out a ship in a day using a succession of quayside teams and a canal as the conveyor belt.

1922

A legacy of its French colonial past, half of Canada drives on the right and the other on the left, but today New Brunswick shifts from the left to the right. British Columbia has already made the transition and the chaos will gradually abate as the other provinces fall into line.

1952

One of the first people to have gender-reassignment surgery, twenty-six-year-old Christine – previously George – Jorgensen, has her story published in the *New York Daily News*. Now an attractive blonde, her story and pictures launch her to international celebrity.

1955

Forty-two-year-old African-American seamstress Rosa Parks refuses to give up her seat to a white man on a bus in Montgomery, Alabama. She is arrested and fined, but becomes the 'Mother of the Civil Rights Movement' as she becomes a rallying point for the African-American protests against discrimination. Their Montgomery Bus Boycott will bring the bus company to near bankruptcy.

2
DECEMBER

1814

Having spent half his life in asylums and prisons, French aristocrat the Marquis de Sade dies. He was involved in the French Revolution when, as a prisoner in the Bastille, he whipped up the mob by screaming from his cell that the prisoners were being tortured to death.

1942

The world's first nuclear chain reaction is instituted with the activation of the first atomic pile by Arthur Compton and Enrico Fermi of the University of Chicago, USA.

1943

Germany bombs the Allied fleet at anchor in Bari, Italy, including the USS *John Harvey*, which is loaded with canisters of mustard gas. Released into water and air, the chemical kills hundreds, but doctors notice that it suppresses some cancerous cells. Nitrogen mustard will become the basis for the first truly effective anti-cancer treatment.

1961

American outlaw Laura Bullion, the longest-surviving member of Butch Cassidy's Wild Bunch, dies in Memphis.

1993

As part of the US War on Drugs, Colombian drug baron and cocaine trafficker Pablo Escobar is caught and shot in Medellín.

3
DECEMBER

1828

Andrew Jackson triumphs over John Quincy Adams in the US presidential election. Jackson's opponents have nicknamed him 'Jackass', which will become the symbol of the Democratic Party.

1920

Having killed nearly 100 million, 5 per cent of the global population, the so-called Spanish Flu pandemic that began in 1918 is on the wane.

1926

English crime novelist Agatha Christie disappears, possibly in an attempt to get her adulterous husband, Archie, arrested for her 'murder'. Leaving her car abandoned in the countryside, she hides in a hotel under a false name for eleven days while the police scour the nation.

1984

A toxic gas leak at the American-owned Union Carbide pesticide plant in Bhopal, India, kills more than 2,000 people on the spot. In the following years many others exposed to the poisonous cloud will also die of its effects and hundreds of thousands will suffer lasting injuries.

1989

US President George Bush and Soviet leader Mikhail Gorbachev end their Malta Summit, promise to halve their nuclear stockpiles and reduce conventional forces in Europe.

4
DECEMBER

1154

Nicholas Breakspear, the only English pope, ascends the papal throne today as Adrian IV. After an unremarkable reign, he will die in 1159, reputedly choking on a fly in his wine.

1674

The Jesuit Jacques Marquette establishes a mission on the shores of Lake Michigan in North America to bring Christianity to the Illiniwek Indians (hence the name 'Illinois'). Unaware that the local name Chicago means stink-weed, in reference to the preponderance of wild garlic growing in the area, he readily accepts the name for his site.

1829

The British Raj outlaws the practice of suttee, or sati, in its territories in India. With women held in low esteem, this is basically a way of un-shouldering the burden of supporting widows by burning them alive on the funeral pyre of their husbands. It is still practised occasionally in rural areas.

2009

Reports in the media reveal that after more than fifty years, the British Ministry of Defence has closed its specialist unit that was set up to monitor the skies for UFOs. This will save more than £45,000 a year, and the Ministry announces wryly that it does not feel that such a cutback will leave the nation vulnerable to extra-terrestrial attack.

5
DECEMBER

1484

Pope Innocent VIII issues a papal bull that recognizes the existence of witches and approves their punishment by the Inquisition. Thousands of people across Europe will be hanged or burned alive in witch-hunts.

1791

Austrian composer Wolfgang Amadeus Mozart dies. According to myth, he dies penniless and is dumped in a communal pauper's grave, but this is a misunderstanding of the practice of the day. To free up burial space in Vienna, everybody apart from the aristocracy is buried in a 'common' grave, which is for an individual but is excavated every ten years.

1933

Prohibition in the US comes to an end with ratification of the Twenty-first Amendment to the Constitution.

1945

Five US Navy aircraft go missing off the Florida coast to start the myth of the Bermuda Triangle. Investigations show that only the leader has navigational instruments and when they malfunction he accidentally leads the flight *away* from land.

6

DECEMBER

1882

English novelist Anthony Trollope dies today. While working for the Post Office, in the 1860s he introduced the bright-red post or pillar boxes for the collection of mail. Unimpressed with this innovation, London's messenger boys allegedly 'post' rats and mice to eat the mail before collection.

1917

Anchored at Halifax, Nova Scotia, the French cargo ship *Mont Blanc*, loaded with high explosives, blows up to flatten everything within a half-mile (800-m) radius. The ship's forward gun is found 3.5 miles (5.6 km) away. About 2,000 are killed.

1956

With the Soviet suppression of the Hungarian Uprising still going on, Hungary meets the USSR in the water polo pool in the Melbourne Olympics for the 'Blood in the Water' match. The game is vicious from the start, with even spectators attempting to join the violence, and is eventually abandoned.

The entire Hungarian team will be granted asylum.

1963

English model and nightclub dancer Christine Keeler begins a nine-month prison sentence for perjury in a previous trial. Her simultaneous affairs with John Profumo, Minister for War, and Yevgeni Ivanov, the Soviet Naval Attaché, caused a scandal. Profumo has already resigned and socialite Stephen Ward has killed himself after being made the scapegoat for the whole affair.

7

DECEMBER

43BC

Tired of vilification from Marcus Tullius Cicero, Roman statesman Mark Antony orders him killed and his head and hands nailed up in the Roman Forum.

1941

So big is the blip-cloud on the Opana Hill radar screens in Hawaii that the operators are told it must be a fleet of American planes and they should ignore it. Instead, it is a wave of Japanese bombers, dive-bombers, torpedo planes and fighters, attacking the US naval base at Pearl Harbor. Japanese pilots leaving the scene after inflicting a direct hit are heard to broadcast 'To-ra', 'surprise achieved', in triplicate, this being misunderstood by American monitors as 'Tora-Tora-Tora', or 'Tiger-Tiger-Tiger'.

1972

Imelda Marcos, First Lady of the Philippines and wife of President Ferdinand Marcos, is giving out prizes for her National Beautification and Cleanliness competition when one of the award-winners, Carlito Dimahilig, whips out a machete and attacks her. She receives wounds that are severe enough to require nearly eighty stitches before Dimahilig is shot dead by bodyguards.

1982

Charles Brooks, a murderer held at Fort Worth Prison, Texas, is the first person to be executed by lethal injection. This method of execution was first suggested in 1888 by New York doctor Julius Bleyer as a cheaper alternative to hanging.

1660

Margaret Hughes appears as Desdemona in Shakespeare's *Othello* at London's Vere Street Theatre, possibly making her England's first professional actress.

1863

At the massive Church of the Company of Jesus in Santiago, Chile, a freak wind rips open the main doors, blows over the altar candles and sucks the doors shut again. Within minutes the place is ablaze and, with all doors opening inwards, the packed congregation is doomed. Up to 3,000 die – the highest death toll of any fire in a single building in history.

1903

English scholar Herbert Spencer dies. It was he, not Charles Darwin, who coined the term 'survival of the fittest' in his *Principles of Botany* (1864). While some will later use it to justify the physically strongest getting their way, the expression actually refers to those species best fitted to their environment, be they big and strong or tiny and fragile.

1920

The last public appearance of Alessandro Moreschi, the last of the Vatican castrati. For centuries, popes have employed surgically modified men who can sing in falsetto to the glory of God. Domenico Mancini, singing in the Vatican until as late as 1959, might also have been a castrato.

9

DECEMBER

1937

In the Second Sino-Japanese War, the Battle for Nanking begins. The Japanese will take the city and give their troops a period of free rein. During this period more than 300,000 Chinese civilians will be raped or murdered.

1967

Nicolae Ceausescu begins his disastrous presidency of Romania.

1979

The eradication of smallpox is announced today with confirmation coming from the World Health Assembly in May next year.

1990

Lech Walesa, founder of the Solidarity union, wins elections to become the first democratically elected president of Poland. Some ten years ago, the American-based company Gillette supposedly offered him $1 million to appear in a commercial shaving off his trademark moustache with their products. He refused.

1992

British Prime Minister John Major announces to a shocked House of Commons and nation that the Prince of Wales and Princess Diana are to separate.

10
DECEMBER

1896

Swedish chemist Alfred Nobel, inventor of dynamite and founder of the Nobel Prizes, dies – for real this time. French newspapers had trumpeted 'The Merchant of Death is Dead' in 1888, having confused him with his brother Ludvig.

1904

Russian physiologist Ivan Pavlov is awarded a Nobel Prize for his famous project with dogs. During his experiment studying digestion, a bell was rung to remind staff to feed the dogs. Reports of them salivating at its ringing prompted Pavlov to look more closely at their reactions to stimuli, and identify the concept of conditioned reflex.

1946

American writer Damon Runyon dies having created characters from New York's Broadway in stories that will later be adapted for the musical *Guys and Dolls*. After his cremation, his ashes will be illegally scattered along Broadway from a small plane flown by American flying-ace Eddie Rickenbacker.

1963

Zanzibar becomes independent from Britain to become a short-lived constitutional monarchy under Jamshid bin Abdullah who will be overthrown within a month. In 1896, Britain and Zanzibar had a thirty-eight-minute war, the shortest in history, during which British gunboats flattened the Imperial Palace.

11
DECEMBER

1792

After the French Revolution, the trial begins of King Louis XVI of France for treason and tyranny. He sits impassively listening to the list of thirty-three charges levelled against him. The vote for his death a foregone conclusion, he will meet Madame Guillotine on 21 January next year.

1963

Having been kidnapped on 8 December, Frank Sinatra, Jr., son of the American singer nicknamed 'Old Blue Eyes', is released in the early hours of this morning by his three kidnappers who, paid $240,000 by his father, dump Frank Junior in Bel Air, Los Angeles. Kidnappers Barry Keenan, John Irwin and Joe Amsler are swiftly rounded up by the FBI.

1964

Argentinian revolutionary Che Guevara addresses the United Nations in New York and is afterwards feted by the cream of American society.

2003

A commission appointed by French President Jacques Chirac reports that all religious symbols should be banned from public schools and buildings. This includes crucifixes, skullcaps, scarves and veils. The ban will become law next year. The commission also recommends that the Jewish day of Yom Kippur and the Islamic holy day of Eid should become formal school holidays.

12
DECEMBER

1098

At the end of a month-long siege during the First Crusade, the occupants of Maarat in Syria are promised safe passage if they surrender. Terms agreed, the Muslims emerge to be slaughtered by the Christians, some of whom, short of food themselves, cook and eat their victims.

1901

Using a box-kite to hoist hundreds of feet of copper wire to act as an aerial, Italian inventor Guglielmo Marconi sends the first transatlantic signal from Newfoundland in Canada to Podhu Wireless Station in Cornwall, England.

1955

His first experiments involving a couple of empty tin cans and a hairdryer, English inventor Christopher Cockerell patents his hovercraft.

1982

Over 30,000 women descend on the US missile base at Greenham Common in Berkshire, UK, to join hands and form a human chain round the base.

1999

Author of the book and the catchphrase *Catch-22*, American writer Joseph Heller dies. Originally titled *Catch-18*, the publication of Leon Uris's recently produced *Mila 18* forced a last-minute change.

13

DECEMBER

1642

The Dutch explorer Abel Tasman sights New Zealand. On 18 December Maori warships row out to meet the pale 'ghosts'. Tasman orders his men to acknowledge them with a jaunty ditty on trumpets, which is interpreted by the Maoris as a war challenge, so his ship is promptly attacked.

1909

With his brother Francis a prime suspect in the theft of the Irish crown jewels, Anglo-Irish explorer Ernest Shackleton is knighted.

1949

The Israeli Parliament, the Knesset, votes to ratify David Ben-Gurion's proclamation of 5 December that Jerusalem should be the capital of Israel. Most countries refuse to move their embassies from Tel Aviv, so most outsiders imagine that is the capital.

2003

Former Iraqi leader Saddam Hussein is arrested by American troops and will face trial and execution for crimes against humanity.

2010

Trouble, the Maltese dog left a $12 million trust fund by American hotelier Leona Helmsley, dies today. In 1989 Helmsley, nicknamed the Queen of Mean, had been given a prison sentence for tax fraud after famously pronouncing that paying taxes was something for little people.

14
DECEMBER

1959

The count from yesterday's election completed, Archbishop Makarios, recently returned from exile, wins a landslide victory to become the first democratically elected president of what will soon become an independent Cyprus.

1973

John Paul Getty III is released by kidnappers after a ransom is paid. The kidnappers demanded $3.2 million but Getty's oil tycoon grandfather refuses in case it makes targets of his other grandchildren. He only relents after the kidnappers cut off the young man's ear and post it to a newspaper. But the tycoon says he will only pay $2.2 million, as this is the maximum he can claim as tax-deductable.

1995

The political leaders of Bosnia, Serbia and Croatia sign the Dayton Accords in Paris to bring an end to three years of bitter conflict in Bosnia, marked by attempts to achieve what has been euphemistically termed 'ethnic cleansing'. Soon the recriminations and war crimes trials will begin.

1999

Former US President Jimmy Carter finishes a job he began in the 1970s when he signed the Torrijos-Carter Treaty, which promised to give control of the Panama Canal to Panama at the end of 1999. Today he officiates at the handover ceremony with all US personnel set to withdraw on 31 December.

15
DECEMBER

1859

Ludwig Lazarus Zamenhof is born in Bialystok, Russia and soon develops multilingual skills. Believing that governments would find it difficult to set nation against nation if we could all speak a common language and understand each other, he will develop Esperanto, meaning 'he who hopes'.

1890

The Native-American chief Sitting Bull is murdered. The victor at the Little Big Horn, he later toured with Buffalo Bill's Wild West Show. Returned to the Standing Rock Reservation in Dakota, he is shot by two Native-American policemen trying to arrest him in case he leads an uprising.

1916

Although sporadic fire will continue until 20 December, the Battle of Verdun in the First World War is effectively over. The first engagement in which the Germans used flamethrowers and storm troopers, more than 250,000 are dead, with the lines of battle pretty much where they were when the fighting started nearly ten months ago.

1944

Headed for France to entertain the troops, American bandleader Glenn Miller's plane disappears in thick fog over the English Channel.

16
DECEMBER

1707
The last eruption of Mount Fuji in Japan.

1773
The Boston Tea Party in the British colony of America is prompted by the British tax on tea and the perceived monopoly of the British East India Company on tea imports. Disguised as Native Americans, protestors board the Company's ships and throw their cargoes of tea overboard.

1850
Under the management of John Sumner, the Archbishop of Canterbury, the first of some 3,500 so-called Canterbury Pilgrims arrive to settle in New Zealand.

1937
Theodore Cole and Ralph Roe become the only two prisoners to break out of prison on Alcatraz Island off San Francisco. Using welded cans as flotation aids, they venture into the violent currents, never to be seen again. The prison governor states that they must have drowned but others are not so sure.

1968
The Second Vatican Council formally rescinds the Vatican's 1492 directive calling for the expulsion of all Jews from Spain.

17
DECEMBER

1849

British soldier Edward Coke, brother of the Earl of Leicester, collects his newly designed riding hat from London hat-makers Thomas and William Bowler. Also known as a derby, the bowler hat is worn in the countryside long before it invades the cities and it will also become the most popular hat in the American West where it finds favour as defensive headgear.

1903

The Wright brothers make their historic first sustained, powered and controlled flight over the sand dunes at Kill Devil Hills on the North Carolina coast; 'kill-devil' was an old name for rum and the location was once a popular landing site for rum smugglers. The brothers then walk four miles to the Kitty Hawk telegraph office to report their success.

1967

Ignoring the advice of friends and bodyguards, Australian Prime Minister Harold Holt goes swimming in heavy surf at Cheviot Beach in Victoria. He disappears and his body is never found.

1989

The Romanian Revolution begins in the city of Timisoara when the army shoots at protestors. Unrest spreads to other cities and on 27 December President Nicolae Ceausescu and his wife, Deputy Prime Minister Elena Ceausescu face a firing squad. Capital punishment is abolished in Romania on 7 January 1990.

18
DECEMBER

1737

Master violin-maker Antonio Stradivari dies in Cremona, Italy. It is estimated that he made about 1,000 instruments in his life, with about 500 of these being violins that are still in use. They are valued at about £1 million each.

1939

The RAF and the Luftwaffe clash in the Battle of the Heligoland Bight, one of the first named engagements of the Second World War. British bombers attack German warships with a loss of twelve planes and fifty-seven aircrew.

1940

Hitler signs the secret Directive 21, giving the go-ahead for Operation Barbarossa, the invasion of Russia, which will begin next summer.

1956

Japan is admitted to the United Nations.

1999

American environmentalist Julia Butterfly Hill ends her 738-day sit-in 180 feet (55 m) up a 1,500-year-old giant redwood in California's Humboldt County. The protest was to guard the tree, nicknamed Luna, from loggers and she only comes down after the lumber company promises to preserve the tree in a 200-foot (61 m) buffer zone.

19
DECEMBER

1848
Having been taken ill during the funeral of her brother, Branwell, who was carried off by a mixture of tuberculosis and alcoholism, Emily Bronte, English author of *Wuthering Heights*, herself dies of tuberculosis at the age of thirty.

1932
Intended as a lifeline to ex-pats around the globe, the BBC launches its Empire Service on the radio. It will be renamed the World Service in 1965.

1972
Ugandan dictator Idi Amin informs the British Government that all British workers in the country should leave or have their pay cut nearly in half.

1984
Britain and China sign the agreement by which the British colony of Hong Kong will be returned to Chinese control in 1997 on condition that the island's unique way of life and economic freedom remain in place for at least fifty years.

2003
Libya's Colonel Gaddafi makes the surprise announcement that he is to destroy his entire arsenal of chemical weapons and those of mass destruction. He also agrees to allow United Nations weapons inspectors into the country.

20
DECEMBER

1915

During the First World War the last ANZAC (Australian and New Zealand Army Corps) troops quietly leave the chaos of Gallipoli with the Turkish Army believing them still in place, thanks to the 'self-firing' rifles invented by Private William Scurry. Hundreds of rifles were rigged with tin cans attached to the triggers by string. Water from other cans dripped into the lower ones until they were heavy enough to pull the trigger.

1973

Spanish Prime Minister Luis Carrero Blanco is killed by an excessively large bomb that hurls his car over the roof of the Church of San Francisco de Borga in Madrid, where the seventy-year-old Blanco had just attended Mass. What is left of the car lands on a second-storey balcony behind the church.

1977

The death of Englishman Henry Tandey VC. During the fighting round Cambrai, northern France, in the First World War, a wounded and exhausted German stumbled out of the smoke in front of him. Reluctant to gun the man down, Tandey gestures him to be on his way. The German soldier was Adolf Hitler.

1989

The US invades Panama to arrest the dictator-drug-baron Manuel Noriega who takes sanctuary in the Apostolic Nunciature, the de facto embassy of the Vatican.

21

DECEMBER

1620

According to popular legend, the passengers of the *Mayflower* land in America, using the so-called Plymouth Rock as a stepping stone. Actually they first put in at Provincetown and the first mention of any rock at Plymouth appears in the 1740s.

1907

More than 2,000 people – striking saltpetre miners and their wives and children – are gunned down by the Chilean Army at Iquique when they refuse to disperse.

1945

US General George S. Patton dies of injuries sustained in a traffic accident in Germany. It is later claimed that Patton's death was arranged by the American and Russian secret services since the general was threatening to blow the whistle on shady deals to do with the division of post-War Europe.

1979

The Lancaster House Agreement, granting recognized independence to Zimbabwe Rhodesia, is signed.

1988

Pan Am Flight 103 is brought down by a bomb over the Scottish town of Lockerbie; all 259 on board are killed along with eleven on the ground. Libyan intelligence officer Abdelbaset al-Megrahi will be convicted of the bombing.

22
DECEMBER

1885

With the end of the Tokugawa Shogunate and the restoration of Imperial power in Japan, the Samurai Ito Hirobumi becomes the first prime minister of the country.

1938

Believed extinct for sixty-five million years, a coelacanth is caught by a South African fisherman.

1975

The Venezulean terrorist Carlos the Jackal and his Palestinian gunmen, together with a group of hostages, are provided with an Austrian Airlines plane to take them from Vienna to Algiers. Yesterday the gang had shot their way into the OPEC Headquarters in Vienna and taken ninety-two hostages, threatening to shoot one every fifteen minutes unless the Austrian Government broadcast a plea for the Palestinian cause on all radio and television networks every two hours. All the hostages are eventually released.

1989

With the barriers between East and West Germany dissolving, the Brandenburg Gate in Berlin is opened for the first time in nearly thirty years. West German Chancellor Helmut Kohl walks through it to shake hands with East German Prime Minister Hans Modrow.

23
DECEMBER

1888

Distraught after arguments with his friend and fellow artist Paul Gauguin, Dutch painter Vincent van Gogh cuts off his left ear before wrapping it in newspaper and taking it to a brothel where, according to the local newspaper, he asks a girl called Rachel to keep it safe.

1948

General Hideki Tojo, ex-Prime Minister of Japan and mastermind of the attack on Pearl Harbor, is hanged for war crimes. He tried to shoot himself in 1945 but was healed in a US Army hospital where he was also given a new set of dentures. The dentist had secretly inscribed the inside of the teeth with 'Remember Pearl Harbor' in Morse code.

1954

Dying of chronic nephritis, twenty-three-year-old American Richard Herrick receives a kidney from his twin, Ronald, in the world's first successful organ transplant. After the five-hour operation carried out in Boston by surgeon Joseph Murray, the patient will survive eight years.

1986

Having taken off from Edwards Air Force Base in California on 14 December, the ultra-light powered glider Voyager touches down again after its non-stop, 26,366-mile (42,432 km) round-the-world flight on a single load of fuel.

24
DECEMBER

1818

The lyrics by a young priest called Joseph Mohr and the tune by Franz Gruber, *Silent Night* is performed for the first time in St Nicholas Church in Oberndorf, Austria. Perennially popular, it will be the song spontaneously sung by British, French and German troops during the 1914 Christmas truce at the trenches.

1914

At Ypres on the Western Front, troops from both sides climb out of their trenches and meet in no-man's-land to exchange family photographs, cigarettes and drinks; they even have a football match. After a few hours, officers on both sides become concerned and come out blowing whistles to get everyone back to killing each other.

1965

A flaming mass arcs over the UK. The meteor, about the size of an office desk, is fortunately shattered into thousands of meteorites by its own sonic boom as it enters the atmosphere to shower the village of Barwell near Leicester. No injuries are reported.

1974

Police in Melbourne, Australia, arrest a man in the street thinking they have found Lord Lucan, who is wanted for murder in Britain. Instead they have caught John Stonehouse, the English MP who has faked his death by drowning in Florida last month to evade debts and to be with his mistress.

25

DECEMBER

1BC

Jesus was not born on this day. The first discussions of today as Christmas appear in the early fourth century when Christians thought it a good idea to fit in with assorted pagan festivals such as Yule. If the shepherds were still out in the fields guarding the sheep at night then the birth must have been lambing time and therefore some time around July or August.

496

Clovis, King of the Franks, is baptized. He abandons his pagan banner featuring golden toads and adopts the Fleur-de-lis. According to one story, in pre-Revolutionary France courtiers at Versailles, harking back to Frankish glory, will refer to themselves as toads and to commoners as frogs, considered lesser creatures. Outsiders pick this up as a blanket term for any Frenchman.

1865

Formed yesterday in Pulaski, Tennessee, the Ku Klux Klan holds its first gathering. The six founding members were classically educated and mainly of Scottish heritage so they based the name on the Greek for circle, and clan.

1880

Charlotte, the German-born wife of British King George III, puts up the first decorated Christmas tree at Windsor.

26
DECEMBER

1890

German archaeologist Heinrich Schliemann dies of an ear infection. In 1871 he identified the site of ancient Troy in Anatolia, now in Turkey.

1972

The death of former American President Harry S Truman – there is no full stop after the S because his middle name was simply 'S'. A keen poker player, he kept a sign on his desk reading 'The Buck Stops Here' because in the Wild West a piece of heavy-gauge buckshot (or in some accounts a knife with a buckhorn handle) marked the poker dealer who 'passed the buck' for the next man to deal.

1982

For the first and only time to date, *Time* magazine's Man of the Year is not human – it is the personal computer.

2004

Following an underwater earthquake, a tsunami smashes into countries bordering the Indian Ocean, killing about 300,000. The tsunami, or harbour-wave, was named centuries ago by Japanese fishermen. At sea a tsunami is flat enough to pass unnoticed under the smallest boat so fishermen returning to find their villages smashed presumed the destructive wave must have originated within the harbour.

27
DECEMBER

537

The Hagia Sophia, or Church of the Holy Wisdom, is completed in Constantinople (Istanbul). With its iconic dome and four needle-towers, it will also function as a mosque until secularized in 1931 to become a museum.

1911

The Jana Gana Mana, India's national anthem, is sung for the first time in Calcutta. With the lyrics praising the 'Dispenser of India's destiny', the Anglo-Indian press mistakenly think the song is in praise of British King George V who is due to arrive on 30 December. It is in fact a reference to Bhagya Vidhata, India's God of Destiny.

1922

Japan launches the *Hosho*, the world's first aircraft carrier.

2006

Boris Gudz, the last surviving combatant of the Russian Revolution of 1917, dies today aged 104. Buried in Moscow with much ceremony, he had in his time been a senior officer of the dreaded OGPU, forerunner of the Russian security agency the KGB.

2007

Pakistani politician and former Prime Minister Benazir Bhutto is assassinated. She is in a bulletproof car, but stands up through the sunroof to wave to the crowds in Rawalpindi.

28
DECEMBER

1734

Rob Roy MacGregor, Highland cattle-thief, blackmailer (in the old sense of extracting protection money) and folk-hero, dies. With extremely long arms, he was a feared swordsman but most of what is 'known' of him comes from the highly coloured and eponymous novel of 1817 by Sir Walter Scott.

1879

Amid a violent storm, the Tay Rail Bridge in Dundee, Scotland, collapses as a train crosses its mid-section. All 300 passengers and crew die. The event is the subject of a poem by Scotsman William McGonagall, who is internationally acclaimed as the worst poet in the English language.

1912

The first San Francisco streetcars go into service today. Still operating with an average speed of eight miles per hour, they form the slowest transit system in America. The most famous streetcar – the one named Desire – ran through New Orleans, from the French Quarter to Desire Street.

2003

In the face of mounting terrorist activity, the UK Government sanctions the use of armed 'sky marshals' to fly undercover on main air routes.

29
DECEMBER

1170

The murder of English Archbishop Thomas Becket in Canterbury Cathedral by four knights who have interpreted a comment by King Henry II as a command to kill the priest.

1860

The world's first iron-hulled, armour-plated warship, Britain's HMS *Warrior*, is launched at Blackwall on the River Thames. Fully restored, she is now berthed at Portsmouth Historic Dockyard along with HMS *Victory* and the Tudor *Mary Rose*.

1890

The last 'battle' between Native Americans and the US Cavalry takes place near Wounded Knee Creek in South Dakota. Surrounding the Lakota Native encampment, 500 soldiers start shooting, killing at least 150 men, women and children.

1929

Radio Luxembourg is granted a licence to broadcast music and news programmes from Luxembourg to Britain and Ireland. It goes on air in 1932. Long a favourite of youth who found the BBC too staid, the station will continue broadcasting in English until 1992.

1998

Violent storms hit the competitors in the Sydney to Hobart yacht race, drowning six.

30
DECEMBER

1916

Russian faith healer and mystic Grigori Rasputin is killed by conspirators in the home of Prince Felix Yusupov in St Petersburg. Some sources say the final shot comes from Captain Oswald Rayner of British Military Intelligence, who has known the prince since they were at Oxford University together. Rasputin had gained enormous influence over the Russian royal family, and Britain was concerned that he was advising the Tsar to withdraw from the First World War. That would have freed 350,000 German troops to return to fight in France.

1922

Russia renames itself the Union of Soviet Socialist Republics.

1973

Teddy Sieff, English businessman and Zionist, has a lucky escape when he is shot in the face by Venezuelan assassin Carlos the Jackal at Sieff's home in London. The bullet bounces off his dentures. Carlos is acting for the Popular Front for the Liberation of Palestine.

2006

Former Iraqi President Saddam Hussein is hanged in Baghdad for crimes against humanity. His last prayers are drowned out by the jeers of those present, one of whom films the execution and posts it on YouTube.

1862

The newly created American state of West Virginia joins the Union. Since half of Virginia had wanted to join, President Abraham Lincoln has simply cut the state into West Virginia and Virginia.

1869

The French painter Henri Matisse is born. In 1961 his *Le Bateau* will hang for forty-seven days in New York's Museum of Modern Art before anyone notices it is displayed upside down.

1948

British speed-king Sir Malcolm Campbell dies with few aware of his help in the D-Day Landings. With it being imperative to find out which parts of Normandy's beaches would take heavy traffic and tanks, Campbell was consulted as to how he tested sand flats for his runs. He supplied the Royal Engineers with his homemade depth-augers, which two men took to France to collect core-samples from under the noses of the German sentries.

1951

Having fought in the 10th Alabama Infantry during the American Civil War and witnessed the surrender of Robert E. Lee at Appomattox, the delightfully named Pleasant Crump, last surviving combatant of the Confederate Army, dies today aged 104.

BIBLIOGRAPHY AND SOURCES

The true list of sources for a book such as this would take up almost as many pages as the book itself. I have trawled through innumerable newspapers, books and websites to reference and crosscheck the entries herein. Sometimes when researching specific dates for events from long ago it is difficult to pinpoint the *exact* day with 100 per cent accuracy, but I have tried to check and recheck all the sources I can find. I would, however, like to acknowledge the invaluable reference sources below:

Encyclopaedia Britannica, various editions
Notes & Queries, online archive, Oxford University Press
The British Newspaper Archive, DC Thompson Family History
On This Day archive, BBC
The History Channel, online archive
Metro News of Toronto, online archive
The History Orb, online archive
Wikipedia

ACKNOWLEDGEMENTS

Thanks to editors Nicola Chalton, Meredith MacArdle, Geoffrey West and Katherine Parker and designer Billy Waqar.

INDEX